U.S. Army
Native American Code Talkers
in World Wars I and II

David M. Sullivan

U.S. Army Native American Code Talkers in World Wars I and II
Copyright © 2017 by David M. Sullivan. All rights reserved.

Designed through 31by5.com
Published and distributed by Lulu.com
ISBN 978-1-387-06714-5

BOOKS BY DAVID M. SULLIVAN:

The United States Marine Corps in the Civil War–The First Year. 1997

The United States Marine Corps in the Civil War–The Second Year. 1997

The United States Marine Corps in the Civil War–The Third Year. 1998

The United States Marine Corps in the Civil War–The Final Year. 2000

The Civil War Uniforms of the United States Marine Corps: The 1859 Regulations, with Lt. Col. Charles H.Cureton. USMCR (Ret.). 2009

BOOKS REVISED AND EDITED BY DAVID M. SULLIVAN:

Biographical Sketches of the Commissioned Officers of the Confederate States Marine Corps. 2003

Dedication

To the Native Americans who wore the uniforms of the United States Army, Marine Corps, Navy, Air Force, and Coast Guard, past and present, in thanks for your service.

Contents

Introduction: U.S. Army Native American Code Talkers	1
Code Talkers in World War I	5
Code Talkers in World War II	37
Tribal Affiliations:	
Cherokee	38
Choctaw Nation	38
Comanche	42
Crow Nation	52
Fond-du-Lac-Band-of-Lake-Superior Chippewa Tribe	54
Hopi	55
Kiowa	57
Menominee	58
Meskwaki (Sac and Fox)	59
Mohawk	62
Muscogee Creek Nation	66
Oneida Nation	67
Osage Nation	68
Pawnee Nation	69
Ponca	71
Pueblo of Acoma	71
Seminoles	72
Great Sioux Nation (Očhéthi Šakówiŋ)	75
Cheyenne River Sioux	77
Crow Creek Sioux	78
Fort Peck Assiniboine Sioux	79
Ho-Chunk Sioux	83
Laguna	84
Oglala Sioux	84
Gen. Douglas Macarthur's Sioux Indian Code Talkers	85
Rosebud Sioux	87
Santee Sioux	89
Sisseton-Wahpeton Sioux	90
Standing Rock Sioux	91
Yankton Sioux	92
Tlingit	93
Unknown Tribal Affiliation	94
Tonto Apache	94
White Mountain Apache	95
Notes	96

David M. Sullivan

Introduction:
U.S. Army Native American Code Talkers

Native Americans have fought gallantly in every conflict since the War for Independence, mostly under the stars and stripes, but some under the stars and bars of the Confederacy. That said, the greatest contribution of Native Americans in wartime was their use as code talkers during World Wars I and II.

The U.S. Marine Corps won acclaim for its extensive use of Navajo code talkers in World War II and a major motion picture, *Wind Talkers,* added to its long list of wartime accomplishments. World War I veteran Philip Johnston proposed the use of Navajo to the Marine Corps at the beginning of World War II. His tests showed Navajo men could encode, transmit, and decode a three-line English message in twenty seconds; the standard method of transmitting the same message took upwards of two minutes. Maj. Gen Clayton B. Vogel, USMC, recommended the Marines recruit two hundred Navajo; the first twenty-nine Navajo recruits entered boot camp in May 1942. The Marine Corps ultimately enlisted some six hundred Navajo for its code talker program. The Navajo code talkers received no recognition until the declassification of the operation in 1968. In 1982, the code talkers were given a Certificate of Recognition by President Ronald Reagan, who also named 14 August 1982 as "Navajo Code Talkers Day." On 21 December 2000, Congress passed, and President William Clinton signed, Public Law 106-554, 114 Statute 2763, which awarded the Congressional Gold Medal to the original twenty-nine World War II Navajo code talkers, and Silver Medals to each person who qualified as a Navajo code talker. Since 1968, numerous books and magazine articles relating to the Navajo code talkers have been published, not to mention the History Channel's frequent interviews with survivors. This being the case, an account of the Navajo code talkers is not covered in this work.

Nationwide, despite the fact between nine thousand and twelve thousand served in combat in France, Native Americans didn't get U.S. citizenship until 1924, years after World War I ended according to the National Museum of the American Indian. They volunteered to fight because defending their land and people was part of their culture and tradition. It was also a sensitive issue for the government. It would have been difficult to explain that the very languages they were trying to eradicate in America had been instrumental in communicating on the battlefield. Until recent years, other Native Americans who were used as code talkers in World Wars I and II remained in relative obscurity, having been sworn to secrecy in addition to their reticence regarding their wartime services—even their parents, siblings, wives, and children were unaware of what they contributed to their country. Although the Navajo code talkers of

World War II received public attention when their code was declassified in 1968, were awarded congressional recognition and gold and silver medals in 2001, all other code talkers remained federally unrecognized.[1] Texas subsequently took action by bestowing the Lone Star Medal of Valor to Choctaw code talkers or their families on 16 September 2007.[2] Then, on 15 November 2008, The Code Talkers Recognition Act of 2008 (Public Law 110-420), was signed into law by President George W. Bush, recognizing every Native American code talker who served in the United States military during World War I or World War II (with the exception of the previously awarded Navajo) with a Congressional Gold Medal, designed as distinct for each tribe, with silver duplicates awarded to the individual code talkers or their next-of-kin. Under The Code Talkers Recognition Act of 2008,[3] Congress recognized the service of these code talkers by authorizing the U.S. Mint to issue a commemorative gold medal, presented on 20 November 2013.

At the time of the medal presentations, a bare handful of code talkers were still alive. These men and those who had passed on, for the most part, kept their wartime services to themselves (apparently at the insistence of the government), thus little more than their names have been recorded. Fortunately, others left something to be preserved for future generations.

David M. Sullivan
Rutland, Massachusetts
2017

Lone Star Medal of Valor, exnet.narod.ruUSA/ngTexas-1

Acknowledgements

Many sources were consulted in the process of this project. Those providing important contributions were, alphabetically: Ladonna Brave Bull Allard; Lanny Asepermy; Robert J. Avery, Detachment Adjutant, Sons of The American Legion, Detachment of New York; Aimée Benedict, Publications Manager / Webmaster, Saint Regis Mohawk Tribe; Gabe Cinquegrana; comanchenation.com; Comanche National Museum and Cultural Center; www.crstvets; dlib.indiana.edu/omeka/mathers/items; fortpecktribes.net; NMAIarchives@si.edu; Mark Ellenbarger; Barbara J. Gotham, 380th Bomb Group Association; Stacy Hutto, Managing Editor, Biskinik, Choctaw Nation Media; Gwenda Elin Gustafson Malnati; nowatamuseum.org; Oklahoma Historical Society; starnews@boreal.org; www.azcentral.com; www.cherokee.org; www.choctawnation.com; www.dday-overlord.com/forum/des-indiens-comanches-ayant-debarque-utah-beach-bientot-commemores-t8119.html; www.findagrave,com; www. www.indianz.com; msswarriors.org; www.okhistory.org; www.reddirtreporrt.com; www.seminolenationmuseum.org; www.soldiers.dodlive.mil.; www.sonsdny.org; and www.welchdakotapapers.com.

Code Talkers in World War I

According to The Children of the Sun Native Culture Web site, "Cherokee was the first Indian language used to transmit a coded message. This was done by the American 30th Infantry Division serving alongside the British during the Second Battle of the Somme." According to the Division Signal Officer, this took place in September 1918 while the Americans were under British command."[4] However, members of the Choctaw Nation who served in the 142d and 143d Infantry Regiments of the 36th Division received more notice and recognition, such as it was, for their work in confounding the Germans.[5]

How the Choctaws came to fame as code talkers was quite by accident. As related by Solomon Bond Louis in 1979:

> It was known that the Germans had "broken" the American radio codes and had tapped the telephone lines. The Germans were also capturing about one out of every four messengers sent out as runners between the various companies on the battle line. One day, Captain Lawrence, commander of one of the companies, was strolling through the company area when he happened to overhear Solomon Louis and Mitchell Bobb conversing in their native Choctaw language. After listening for a few minutes, he called Lewis and asked, "Corporal, how many of you Choctaws do we have in this battalion?" After a conference with Bobb, Louis told the Captain, "We have eight men who speak fluent Choctaw in the Battalion, Sir." "Are there any of them over in headquarters Company?" the Captain asked. "I think Carterby and Maytubby are over there, Sir'" Louis replied. "You fellows sit right here," said the Captain. He got on the field telephone and discovered that, indeed, Ben Carterby and Pete Maytubby (whose father, Peter Maytubby, Sr., served in the 1st Volunteer Cavalry under Teddy Roosevelt and fought in the Spanish-American War) were attached to Headquarters Company. "Get them and have them stand by," Captain Lawrence told his commanding officer, "I've got an idea that might just get those Heinies off our backs." Calling Louis and Bobb, the Captain told them, "Look, I'm going to give you a message to call in to headquarters and I want you to give the message in your language. There will be somebody there who can understand it." It was at that moment that Pfc. Mitchell Bobb, using a field telephone, delivered the first Choctaw code message to Choctaw Ben Carterby, who then translated it into English for the battalion commander. (Solomon Louis chose seven other Choctaws who served as code

Cpl. Solomon Bond Louis (1899–1972). *Bishinik*, The Official Monthly Publication of the Choctaw Nation of Oklahoma, Durant, OK.

Pvt. Mitchell Bobb. *Bishinik*.

talkers and was apparently appointed chief of detail.[6]) Within a matter of hours, the eight men able to speak the Choctaw language had been shifted until there was at least one in each field company headquarters. Not only were they handling field telephone calls, they were translating radio messages into the Choctaw Language and writing field orders to be carried by "runners" between the various companies.[7]

The situation can be best told in the words of Colonel A. W. Bloor,[8] the commander of the 142d Infantry Regiment. The memo he sent to the Headquarters read:

> Headquarters 142nd Infantry, A.E.F.
> January 23, 1919, A.P.O. No. 796

From: C.O. 142nd Infantry
To: The Commanding General 36th Division (Attention Capt. Spence)
Subject: Transmitting messages in Choctaw

1. In compliance with memorandum, Headquarters 36th Division, January 21, 1919, to C.O. 142nd Infantry, the following account is submitted

In the first action of the 142nd Infantry at St. Etienne, it was recognized that of all the various methods of liaison the telephone presented the greatest possibilities. The field of rocket signals is restricted to a small number of agreed signals. The runner system is slow and hazardous. T.P.S. is always an uncertain quantity. It may work beautifully and again, it may be entirely worthless. The available means, therefore, for the rapid and full transmission of information are the radio, buzzer and telephone, and of these the telephone was by far the superior,—provided it could be used without let or hindrance,—provided straight to the point information could be given.

It was well understood however, that the German was a past master of "listening in" moreover, from St. Etienne to the Aisne we had traveled through a county netted with German wire and cables. We established P.C.s in dugouts and houses, but recently occupied by him. There was every reason to believe every decipherable message or word going over our wires also went to the enemy. A rumor was out that our Division had given false coordinates of our supply dump, and that in thirty minutes the enemy shells were falling on the point. We felt sure the enemy knew too much. It was therefore necessary to code every message of importance and coding and decoding took valuable time.

While comparatively inactive at Vaux-Champagne, it was remembered that the regiment possessed a company of Indians. They spoke twenty-six different languages or dialects, only four or five of which were ever written. There was hardly one chance in a million that Fritz would be able to translate these dialects and the plan to have these Indians transmit telephone messages was adopted. The regiment was fortunate in having two Indian officers who spoke several of the dialects. Indians from the Choctaw tribe were chosen and one placed in each P.C.

The first use of the Indians was made in ordering a delicate withdrawal of two companies of the 2d Bn. from Chufilly to Chardoney on the night of October 26th. This movement was completed without mishap, although it left the Third Battalion, greatly depleted in previous fighting, without support. The Indians were used repeatedly on the 27th in preparation for the assault on Forest Farm. The enemy's complete surprise is evidence that he could not decipher the messages.

After the withdrawal of the regiment to Louppy-le-Petit, a number of Indians were detailed for training in transmitting messages over the telephone. The instruction was carried on by the Liaison Officer Lieutenant Black. It had been found that the Indian's vocabulary of military terms was insufficient. The Indian for "Big Gun" was used to indicate artillery. "Little gun shoot fast", was substituted for machine gun and the battalions were indicated by one, two and three grains of corn. It was found that the Indian tongues do not permit verbatim translation, but at the end of the short training period at Louppy-le-Petit, the results were very gratifying and it is believed, had the regiment gone back into the line, fine results would have been obtained. We were confident the possibilities of the telephone had been obtained without its hazards.

W. Bloor, Colonel
142d Infantry
Commanding.[9]

However, there is another view of how the Choctaw were tasked with using their language to send messages over tapped telephone lines. According to Mozelle Dawson of Coalinga, California, her father, Albert Billy, suggested the Choctaw language be used to confuse the enemy to his commanding officer.

She said Billy had the idea Indians be used on the phone lines talking in their native dialect. This would confuse anyone tapping into the lines. As it turned out, the Germans were more than just a little confused, and after the Choctaw Code Talkers were put on the phones, the Germans immediately began losing. Ms. Dawson said her father told her that during the night, some Germans were captured, and a general of the German Army said he would like to ask just one question: "What nationality was on the phones that night?" The only reply this German officer received was it was only Americans that had been on the phones.[10]

Capt. Ben H. Chastaine, a company commander of the 142d Infantry, later wrote:

> In the preparations of the 142d for the attack, novel scheme of keeping the movements of the troops secret was worked out. The entire country was covered by a network of abandoned German wires which were suspected of having been left purposely in such a condition that the enemy across the river could connect up with them and "listen in" to the messages being transmitted to various parts of the American lines. More than once there had been evidence to indicate that such things had been accomplished. To overcome this condition, Colonel Bloor selected some of the most intelligent Indians from Company E, composed almost entirely of redmen for Oklahoma and stationed them at the telephones. These Indians were members of the Choctaw tribe and when the messages

Pvt. Albert Billy.
www.choctawnation.com.

Cpl. Tobias William Frazier (1892–1975). Frazier was wounded in action and received the Purple Heart. Oklahoma Historical Society, Oklahoma City, OK.

Pvt. Robert Taylor. www.reddirtreport.com.

Pvt. Benjamin Wilburn Hampton (1892–1963) www.reddirtreport.com.

were handed to them in English, they transmitted them in their own tongue and it is reasonably assured that no word of this was picked up by the Huns.[11]

Nineteen men were recruited to transmit messages and devise a system of communications for the code Talkers: ranging in age from nineteen to thirty-four, the code talkers from the 142d were: Cpl. Solomon Bond Louis, Company E; Pvt. Ben Carterby, Company E; Pvt. Robert Taylor, Company E ; Pvt. Benjamin W. Hampton; Sgt. Tobias William Frazier, Company E and Headquarters Company; Pvt. Mitchell Bobb, Company E; Cpl. Calvin Wilson, Company E; Cpl. Pete Maytubby, Company E; Cpl. James M. Edwards, Company E; Pvt. Jeff Nelson, Company E; Pfc. Albert Billy, Company E; Capt. Columbus Walter Veach, Company E; Pvt. Joseph Davenport; Pfc. George Davenport; Pvt. Noel Johnson; Pvt. Benjamin Colbert, Jr.; Cpl. Otis Leader. Cpl. Victor Brown, Headquarters Company, 143d; and Pfc. Joseph Oklahombi, Company D, 141st.[12] All performed their duty at the front heroically, but of this

Cpl. Otis Leader (1882–1961). For his valor, Leader received a Purple Heart, two Silver Stars, the Distinguished Service Cross, nine battle stars and two individual awards of the Croix de Guerre, France's highest military honor. www.findagrave.com.

number, only a few accounts of their battlefield service have been recorded. Of these few, Cpl. Otis Leader was the most recognized.

Otis Leader was born near Citra in Hughes County, Oklahoma, on 5 November 1882, and entered the Army at the age of thirty-five, one of the oldest men in the service. He was 34 when he joined the Army. He and his Swiss employer from his job on a ranch near Allen, Oklahoma, went on a cattle-buying trip to Fort Worth. The Swiss accent of Leader's employer, combined with the tall, dark looks of the 34 year old resulted in the mistaken pegging of them as a German spy and his Spaniard companion. This mistaken identity infuriated Leader so much he immediately went to the nearest recruiting office and signed up. Upon his arrival in France, Leader was selected to pose as the model representative of the newly arrived American soldiers by a French artist commissioned to paint portraits of the Allied army by the French government. His portrait and statue are in Paris and London. Leader was a member of Company B, 2d Machine Gun Battalion, 16th Infantry Regiment, 1st Infantry Division. He was awarded the French Croix de Guerre twice, a Purple Heart, and Citation Stars (later revised to two Silver Stars) for Sommerviller, Ansauville, Picardy, Cantigny,

Second Marne, St. Mihiel, Meuse-Argonne, Mouson-Sedan, and Coblenz Bridgehead, Leader was called one of the "war's greatest fighting machines" by General Pershing. On the night of 2 November 1917, Leader's company drew the first relief assignment, moving into the trenches at Bathlemont. The following day his company defended the flank in the first engagement of Americans in combat of World War I. On 28 May 1918, Leader was wounded and gassed during the American offensive at Cantigny but rejoined his division near Soissons in July. In the next battle, he crawled through a ravine to attack a machine gun nest. Getting within sixty feet of the enemy, Leader picked up a rifle and fought with the infantry after his own machine gun crew had all been killed. Attacking the German positions, Leader captured two machine guns and eighteen enemy soldiers manning them. On 1 October 1918, he was wounded again and hospitalized at Vichy. He was still in the hospital when the armistice was signed on 11 November.[13]

Joseph Oklahombi, whose surname means "man-killer," born in 1892, has been lauded as Oklahoma's greatest hero of World War I.

> A month before the armistice in 1918, Oklahombi and his comrades in Company D, 141st Infantry, 36th Division, were cut off from the rest of the company. They came across a German machine gun emplacement with about fifty trench mortars. Crossing 'No Man's Land' numerous times, the Choctaw warrior assisted his wounded friends and carried information back to headquarters about the enemy. Oklahombi moved about 200 yards over open ground against artillery and machine gun fire, rushing a machine gun nest and capturing one of the guns. Turning the weapon on the enemy, the Americans held the Germans down with blistering fire for four days until their surrender. Of the enemy, 171 were taken prisoner. On another occasion, Oklahombi confronted a German troop having a meal and resting in a cemetery. Enclosed by high walls with only one gate, Oklahombi covered the gate with blistering fire. A true marksman, Oklahombi killed the Germans by the dozens, seventy-nine according to some reports, until the whole force surrendered.[14]

General orders cited Oklahombi for his bravery for his actions. He was awarded the Citation Star (from 1932, Silver Star) to be worn on the Victory Ribbon by General Pershing. General orders cited Oklahombi for his bravery in moving about 200 yards of open territory, braving machine gun and artillery fire. He received the Croix de Guerre from Marshall Henri Petain:

> Under a violent barrage, [Pvt. Oklahombi] dashed to the attack of an enemy position, covering about 210 yards through barbed-wire

Pfc. Joseph Oklahombi (1895–1960) wearing the Croix de Guerre.
www.reddirtreport.com.

entanglements. He rushed on machine-gun nests, capturing 171 prisoners. He stormed a strongly held position containing more than 50 machine guns, and a number of trench mortars. Turned the captured guns on the enemy, and held the position for four days, in spite of a constant barrage of large projectiles and of gas shells. Crossed no man's land many times to get information concerning the enemy, and to assist his wounded comrades.

He was the most-decorated soldier from Oklahoma during World War I.

Victor Brown, one of the original Choctaw code talkers of World War I, served in the 143d Infantry. His daughter, Napanee Brown Coffman said of his wartime experience:

> He was one of the Indian telephone operators who spoke Choctaw. The Germans could not break the code. He served in the Meuse-Argonne Offensive and was wounded (as his citation from President Wilson states)—gassed (mustard gas), broken nose and head injuries. My father seldom talked about the war, but I used to ask him and he would tell me about his war service and experiences. I remember quite well about his stories of speaking in Choctaw over the telephone lines as he was very proud and pleased that they had 'fooled the Germans.' He was also very pleased to have served in France and to have seen Paris because he was one-fourth French and three-quarters Choctaw.[15]

Pfc. Victor Brown and wife. *Bishinik*.

James Edwards was a member of the Choctaw language "relay team" for messages, and also helped work out the code words to use in the transmissions. "Twice big group" in Choctaw was used for battalion, "eight group" was a squad, "scalps" were casualties, "fast shooting gun" meant machine gun and "big gun" was field artillery. He also chose eight other Choctaw men who spoke the native language fluently to help develop the code. In addition to the above, they used Choctaw words to relay positions and information. For instance, second battalion was "tanch nihi tuklo," or "two grains of corn"; ammunition was "uski

Cpl. James Edwards. www.choctawnation.com.

naki," or "arrow"; attack was "ittibbi," or "fight." Edwards was reportedly the first to transmit messages in Choctaw on 26 October 1918. Later during World War II, he tried to enlist again, stating "maybe they [German forces] still can't talk Choctaw." [16]

Solomon Bond Louis was actually underage when he entered the armed services. This young Bryan County Choctaw attended Armstrong Academy and when his older friends enlisted, Louis pretended to be 18 so that he, too, could join. Louis is credited with being the leader of the original Choctaw Code Talkers in World War I. He received his basic training at Fort Sill, Oklahoma and then was sent to Fort Worth, Texas where he joined an all-Indian Company which was part of the 36th Division. Louis was stationed at division headquarters, with Choctaw James Edwards on the other end of the telephone line with the field artillery. With Edwards in the actual combat zone, he was able to inform Louis, using the Choctaw language, what the Germans were up to.[17]

Walter Veach helped organize Company H, 1st Infantry (Durant, Oklahoma's first National Guard unit) and served as its commander. Under his command, Company H put down the Crazy Snake uprising near Henryetta in the old Creek Nation and later was detailed to patrol the border between the United States and Mexico. The company had a major hand in stopping the Pancho Villa invasion of Texas. In 1917, the company merged with the Texas 36th Division and was sent to Europe. Veach, now a captain, was told to organize an all-Indian company of members of eleven Oklahoma Indian tribes. This all-Indian company was Company E. The company saw much activity during the war, and received recognition for the use of Indian language as a "code" to confound the Germans who were tapping in on their field telephone lines.[18]

Solomon Bond Louis.
www.reddirtreport.com.

Capt. Walter Veach (1884–1956). Veach's given name was Columbus. He enlisted in Company H, 1st Oklahoma Infantry in August 1908 and reached the rank of captain before the United States entered the war. Oklahoma Historical Society, Oklahoma City, OK.

Pvt. Ben Carterby (1893–1953).
www.reddirtreport.com.

Ben Carterby embraced the unpretentious, quiet existence of an ordinary man in private life. Determined not to remember the war and the fighting, he purposely avoided discussions and nostalgic memories of the frightening experiences of war, a common thread among all veterans.

Although the Choctaw code talkers were promised medals for their exceptional wartime service, none were awarded. During the annual Choctaw Labor Day Festival in 1986, Chief Hollis E. Roberts presented posthumous Choctaw Nation Medals of Valor to the families of the Code Talkers. This was the first official recognition the Choctaw Code Talkers had been given.[19]

Choctaw Medal of Valor World War I. *Bishinik*.

Pvt. Noel Johnson, www.reddirtreport.com.

U.S. Army Native American Code Talkers in World Wars I and II   21

Choctaw Nation Code Talkers Medal. The obverse design (left) features a soldier on his field phone writing TANAMPO CHITO, which translates to "big gun" in the Choctaw language. Inscriptions are CHOCTAW NATION and CODE TALKERS. The reverse design (right) features the major elements from the Choctaw Nation seal, identified as the pipe hatchet and bow and arrows. Inscriptions are WORLD WAR I, WORLD WAR II and ACT OF CONGRESS 2008 www.usmint.gov/mint_programs/medals/?action=codeTalkers.

George Adair was one soldier named as a code talker from the Cherokee Nation. After basic training, Adair was assigned to the 36th Division. Adair, along with other Cherokees, was put in the telephone service. It was the Cherokee soldiers' responsibility to receive and transmit crucial orders in their native language. "There was also a group of Cherokee soldiers in the telephone service who disconcerted Germans by transmitting orders in their native language."[20] Unfortunately, none of that group has been identified and only Adair's name remains known among the Cherokee who performed code talking services.[21]

Pvt. George Adair (1887–1947), Cherokee Code Talker. nowatamuseum.org.

Choctaw "Telephone Squad" at Camp Devens, Massachusetts. Wannamaker Collection W64. 51, William Hammond Mathers Museum, Indiana University, Indianapolis, IN. L-R, Cpl. Solomon B. Louis, Pvt. Mitchell Bobb, Cpl. Calvin Wilson, Cpl. James Edwards, Sr., Pvt. George Davenport and Capt. E. H. Horner. www.choctawnation.com.

Soldiers from other tribes acted as code talkers. Comanche Calvin Atchavit, Gilbert Pahdi Conwoop, Edward Albert Nahquaddy Sr., Samuel Tabytosavit, and George Clark are listed as code talkers. In 1918, George Clark, one of the five Comanche who used their native tongue to perplex the Germans, recalled, "There were two or three Choctaw boys who were in the same outfit, sitting and talking to each other in their native tongue. An officer came by and heard them talking. The thought came to him that these boys talking in their native tongue, the Germans wouldn't be able to understand it. ... The Germans never did figure it out." Albert Nahquaddy, Sr. told his son he and other Comanche used their native language during World War I.[22] Haddon Codynah, a Comanche code talker who served in World War II, recalled listening to the Comanche veterans of the war as they spoke of how they and men of other tribes were

Pvt. Gilbert Pahdi Conwoop (1894–1974.) was wounded in action and gassed but did not go to a hospital. He returned to the United States on 11 May 1919 after occupation duty in Germany. Photo courtesy of Lanny G. Asepermy, Sergeant Major, U.S. Army (Ret.), Historian for the Comanche Indian Veterans Association and the Comanche Nation Museum.

Pvt. Edward Albert Nahquaddy Sr. (1894–1974.) was one of the first Comanche to enlist during World War I on 24. February 1918. He trained at Camp Gordon, Georgia, Newport News, Virginia and Camp Travis, Texas. Private Nahquaddy was wounded in action and gassed but did not go to a hospital. He returned to the United States on 11 May 1919. Photo courtesy of Lanny G. Asepermy.

used as code talkers.[23] Messages in Choctaw or later in Comanche were never decoded."[24]

Calvin Atchivit was drafted into the U.S. Army in May 1918, and assigned to the 357th Infantry Regiment at Camp Travis, Texas, on 18 May 1918. On 12 September 1918, Private Atchavit was serving with Company A, 357th Infantry Regiment, 90th Division, American Expeditionary Forces, and saw action during the Battle of Saint-Mihiel, near Fey-en-Heye, France. Despite being severely wounded, for his valorous actions that day he was awarded the Army's second highest award for valor, the Distinguished Service Cross. Distinguished Service Cross Citation:

> The Distinguished Service Cross is presented to Calvin Atchavit, Private, U.S. Army, for extraordinary heroism in action near Fey-en-Heye, France, 12 September 1918. During the attack of his company, though he had been severely wounded in his left arm, Private Atchavit shot and killed one of the enemy and captured another. General Orders 87, W.D., 1919.

Pvt. Calvin (Nahato) Atchivit (1893–1943) shown here wearing his Distinguished Service Cross and the Belgian Croix de Guerre. He was also awarded the Purple Heart and the WW I Victory Medal. Photo courtesy of Lanny G. Asepermy.

Pvt. Samuel Tabytosavit (1896–1970) was treated for severe trench foot in Hospital 202 in Orleans, France, and returned to the United States after occupation duty in Germany on 10 June 1919. Photo courtesy of Lanny G. Asepermy.

Pvt. George Clark (1896–1944.) was most likely drafted in May 1918 and was an infantryman. He was neither wounded or gassed and returned to the United States on 22 June 1919 after occupation duty in Germany and was discharged on 17 July 1919. Photo courtesy of Lanny G. Asepermy.

Achavit was also awarded the Belgian War Cross by the Belgian Government for his services as a Comanche code talker on the field phones during the fighting when the Germans were tapping the lines and trying to intercept Army messages. His use of the Comanche language helped the Allied Army send messages that German ears could not understand. He returned to the United States on 5 June 1919 and discharged on 16 June 1919.[25]

The largest number of Native Americans from a single tribe and who are listed as code talkers in World War I came from the Standing Rock Sioux: Alphonse Bear Ghost, Roscoe White Eagle, Julius Bear Shield, Louis Big Horn Elk, Richard Blue Earth, John Brave Bull, August Brought Plenty, John Brought Plenty, Albert Grass, Joseph Gray Day, Joseph Pretends Eagle, John Elk, Paul Good Iron, Thomas Gray Bull, , George Jacob Halsey, Michael Halsey, Charles Little Chief, George Many Wounds, William Menz, David Molash, George Molash, Thomas Crow Necklace, Louis Crow Skin, John Red Bean, George James Red Fox, Asa Red Stone, George W. Santee, Lawrence See the Elk, George Sleeps from Home, Clyde Standing Bear, James Tattoed, Alexander Traversie, George Two Bears, Joseph Two Bears, Edward Two Horses, Luke

Cherokee Nation Code Talkers Medal. The obverse design (left) features a code talker communicating on a field phone and writing in the Cherokee language. Inscriptions are CHEROKEE NATION and CODE TALKERS in both Cherokee Syllabary and English. The reverse design (right) features a variation of the Cherokee Nation seal. Inscriptions are WORLD WAR I, WORLD WAR II and ACT OF CONGRESS 2008. www.usmint.gov/mint_programs/medals/?action=codeTalkers.

Speaks Walking, Richard White Eagle, Paul White Lightning, Frank Young Bear, Francis Benjamin Zahn, Benjamin Gray Hawk and Harvey E. Lean Elk, and Harry E. Lean Elk.

Very little information has been located with regard to the service of code talkers from the Standing Rock Sioux in World War I. However, some details of their experiences in combat have been preserved. Cpl. Alphonse Bear Ghost served in Co. M, 26th Infantry Regiment, 1st Infantry Division. One of "Pershing's Own," he was wounded in the left arm during the Battles of Montididier and St. Mihiel. Bear Ghost was awarded the Citation Star for bravery during the Argonne Forest fighting. His sergeant said of him: "I wished many times that all the boys in the American Army were like Bear Ghost."[26] Richard Blue Earth volunteered in Company I, 2d North Dakota Volunteer Infantry on 2 August 1917 and was assigned to Company A, 18th Infantry Regiment, 1st Infantry Division, 3d Army. He became a noted sniper. He was killed 11 October 1918 south of Sedan in the Argonne Forest, France.[27]

Pvt. Edward Two Horses, recollected:

> I was with the A.E.F. 90th Division, landed in France, 7 July 1918. We were in the front line trenches in August this line called Toul Sector. Then we stayed there until the big drive began on September 12–18. We went over the top in early in morning before the sun rise up. I was a battalion runner. I went through the machine gun bullet whizzle & shell burstered and German air plane dropping bombs at

Pfc. Alphonse Bear Ghost (1896–1972) served in Company M, 26th Infantry Regiment, 1st Infantry Division, was wounded, left arm, at Argonne Forrest Service—Montididier, St. Mihiel—and cited for bravery: "Headquarters 2nd Infantry Brigade. American Forces in Germany. Montabaur, Germany, 12 July 1919. General orders No 6} The Brigade Commander cites the following officers and men for gallantry in action and devotion to duty during the operations of 2nd Infantry Brigade, American Expeditionary Forces, France, 1917. 1918: Pfc. Alphonse Bear Ghost, 55085, Company M. 26th Infantry. A soldier of splendid qualities of courage and bravery. During the St. Mihiel Offensive, September 12. 13, 1918. displayed great gallantry and devotion to duty. By command of Brigadier General Bumford, George J. Foster, Captain Infantry, Acting Brigade Adjutant." Bear Ghost wears Silver Star for citation—Argonne Forrest. Photographed on his return from France at Camp Merritt, New Jersey. dlib.indiana.edu/omeka/mathers/items.

Pvt. Richard Blue Earth (1893–1918) was the first Native American from North Dakota to enlist. He volunteered in Company I, 2d North Dakota Volunteer Infantry on 2 August 1917. Served in Company A, 18th U. S. Infantry, 1st Division, 3d Army. Blue Earth became a noted sniper and, in the performance of this duty, died with a German bullet between the eyes on 11 October 1918, somewhere south of Sedan in the Argonne Forest. www.welchdakotapapers.com.

Pvt. Edward Two Horses www.welchdakotapapers.com.

Pvt. John Brave Bull. Courtesy of LaDonna Brave Bull Allard.

Pvt. Albert Grass (–1918), Company A, 18th Infantry Regiment, 1st Infantry Division, was killed by shellfire in July 1918. www.welchdakotapapers.com.

Pvt. Charles Little Chief.
www.welchdakotapapers.com

U.S. Army Native American Code Talkers in World Wars I and II   33

Pvt. Francis Benjamin Zahn Company G, 351st Infantry Regiment, 88th Infantry Division. www.welchdakotapapers.com.

Pvt. Harvey Lean Elk with his comrade Pvt. Ben Grey Hawk.
www.welchdakotapapers.com.

us but I never get a scratch to get by with it. The next morning I was lost in the wood I don't know where I was at. I thought myself I was in German ground or no man's land but after finally I know where I was. After a week later I was gassed because my mask is torn by surprise big shell explosion.[28]

The only newspaper account of Sioux code talkers in World War I is an article from the *Steubenville [Ohio] Gazette* under the title, "Played Joke on the Huns: Sioux Indians Had Fun for Three Days Talking over a Tapped Telephone Wire":

> Because of the nature of the country over which American troops fought in the Meuse-Argonne offensive, the Germans found it easy at times to cut in on our field telephone wires. The commander of one brigades attached to an American Division was particularly annoyed by enemy wire tappers in a heavily wooded section of the Argonne. Code messages from artillery observers were being intercepted by Boche listeners-in and the commanders knew, as all armies know, that no code is impregnable when experts get working on it. … Two Indians, both of proud Sioux heritage, members of one of his company[s], were assigned as telephone operators. One was to go forward with the artillery observer, the other to remain at the brigade receiving end of the wire which the artillery captain was certain the Germans had that day tapped somewhere along the line. Now, when the two Sioux Indians get talking together in their own tongue, what they say sounds very much like code, but isn't. Anyway, it raised hob with the code experts of certain Prussian guard units. The Sioux stuck on their jobs for three days and nights. They and the artillery commander and their own colonel enjoyed the situation immensely. If the Germans got any fun out of it they kept it to themselves.[29]

Osage tribesmen served as the telephone messengers in the 36th Division and "used to love to talk on our telephones and they'd talk in Osage. We used to wonder if the Germans could ever interpret those calls." If the Germans could, two white 36th veterans, Wendell Martin and Alphonzo Bulz, remarked "it would have confused the hell out of them." Augustus Chouteau is the only Osage identified as a code talker.[30] "My grandmother told me that those boys [Osage enlisted] spoke to each other over there in the native language so no one could understand them. It was one of the few things I knew about my grandfather and I made sure to tell all my daughters," said Frances Chouteau Jones, his granddaughter.[31]

Other Native Americans served as code talkers (names of the few identified as such precede tribal affiliation) during World War I, including: Cheyenne; Akwesasne Mohawk; Brule Sioux—Willie Iron Elk and Moses Elk Horn; Cheyenne River Sioux; Ho-Chunk Sioux; Meskwaki; Pawnee; Ponca Sioux; Guy George Chapman; Santee Sioux; Tonto Apache; and Yankton Sioux.[32] Unfortunately, no information concerning any of these men has come to light.

None of the Native Americans were assigned to duty specifically as code talkers—the term not coming into use until World War II—since no formal codes were established. They conversed with fellow tribesmen by telephone in situational circumstances and when it became an operational necessity. As Lawrence Stallings wrote in, *The Doughboys: The Story of the AEF, 1917-1918*, "No secrecy was needed by telephone talkers. Who among the enemy understood the Choctaw tongue?"[33] Or for that matter, any of the languages spoken by any Native American tribe?

Code Talkers in World War II

The Germans knew about the successful use of code talkers during World War I and sent a team of some thirty anthropologists to the United States to learn Native American languages in the years before the outbreak of World War II.[34] George Clark, the Comanche code talker from World War I, remembered of the Germans, "They began to infiltrate and try to buy their way in to the elderly Comanche who spoke the old tongue."[35] It proved too difficult for them to learn the many languages and dialects that existed. Forrest Kassanavoid, a Comanche code talker of World War II stated,

> Back in about 1939, some Germans came to the United States to study anthropology at Columbia University. They came out here to a German missionary church near Indiahoma to study native languages. They didn't look like students to us—they were in their 30s. We were told later that just at the end of summer, they were all arrested. We heard the FBI came in and arrested them.[36]

Because of the German anthropologists' efforts to learn the languages being under consideration, the U.S. Army did not implement a large-scale code talker program in the European Theater of the war. Prejudice also played a role preventing the implementation of a wide scale program such as the Marine Corps initiated. Despite the World War I successful use of code talkers, Native Americans were considered intellectually deficient to justify efforts to train them as such. One study claimed, "this idea was 'tried with little success in World War I, but it is thought that official records would disclose the idea was suggested and discarded as impractical and dangerous, not only from the standpoint of security, but also from the standpoint of accuracy."[37] However, there were some in the Army who remembered how effective the code talkers had been during World War I as America's entry into World War II loomed on the horizon in 1940 and 1941. According to William Meadows, author of *The Comanche Code Talkers of World War II* (Austin: University of Texas Press, 2003), the Army first recruited 17 Oneida-Chippewa in the fall of 1940, followed by 17 Comanche and 8 Meskwaki over the next few months, and 8 Hopi in 1943. While small groups of soldiers from other tribes would go on to use their native languages for secure communications throughout the war, the Army Signal Corps specifically trained soldiers from these four tribes in field communication; to be wire linemen and operators; teletype operators; switchboard operators; radio operators; and motor messengers as well as code talkers.

Tribal Affiliations

Cherokee

Despite efforts to locate information regarding the Cherokee honored as code talkers during World War II, their names remain unknown.[38]

Choctaw Nation

The Choctaw Nation sent many of its sons to the armed forces during World War II, four of whom served in the Army as code talkers: 2d Lt. Schlicht Billy, Pfc. Forrester Baker, Cpl. Andrew Perry (died of wounds, 20 August 1944), and Sgt. Davis Pickens, all of whom served in Company K of the 180th.

Schlicht Billy served with the 180th Infantry Regiment, 45th Infantry Division, enlisted as a private in the U.S. Army, rose through the ranks to platoon sergeant, and received a battlefield commission as a second lieutenant. He took part in the Anzio landing; the liberation of Rome; the landings in southern France; and was awarded the Silver Star with Oak Leaf Cluster and the Purple Heart with three Oak Leaf Clusters. Lieutenant Billy was the last surviving Choctaw code talker, passing away on 10 January 1994. Baker, Perry, and Pickens also served with the 180th Infantry. When asked about his use of his native language, Billy replied,

> We were more of an experiment because we had it at hand right there. When a shell hits, it tears up your communication lines—so we had these little 536 radios. I went to school for that, so I had knowledge on how to use that. And we knew that the Germans were good at breaking codes and tying into our lines, things like that. So that was the fastest and easiest and we had the language.[39]

Billy said he regularly conversed in Choctaw, usually with his friend Davis Pickens, fellow Choctaw and platoon machine gunner, providing exact details regarding enemy targets without risking interception by the Germans.[40] Pickens relayed the information he got from Schlicht to the appropriate destination in English, bringing artillery, tanks, close aerial support, or even naval gunfire to the coordinates provided.

Maj. Jack L. Treadwell, battalion commander in the 180th Infantry Regiment, recalled of Lieutenant Billy being the first to crack a portion of the vaunted Siegfried Line.

> We'd been attacking since 15 March, but it was not until the night of the seventeenth that we found ourselves right up against the buzz

2d Lt. Schlicht Billy. *Bishinik*.

saw of what the Germans hoped and believed was an impregnable defense. The Siegfried Line was composed of a great number of reinforced concrete pillboxes, so placed as to support and defend each other linked together by head high trenches. The concrete of those fortifications was six feet thick. The apertures through which the machine guns fired were screened by three quarter inch armor plates against which, we were to discover, rifle grenades were ineffective. Above ground the pillboxes appeared to be only low mounds of earth, and they were so cleverly camouflaged that you could be standing right on top of one and never know it.

The night of the seventeenth we received new maps, together with such data as G2 had been able to gather about the Siegfried defenses- which wasn't much. It was quite clear that the next day we'd be called upon to make "the run for the roses." In the circumstances, therefore, I was forced to take a very dim view of Pete's load of liberated liquor. Not a single bottle is to be opened! I ordered, and that's the way it was. When we swept forward the next morning, we left behind us fifteen cases of choice spirits, a situation calculated to break any soldier's heart.

We shoved off about 0600 and encountered only light resistance until noon, by which time we'd fought our way up to and through the little town of Assweiler. Once beyond the town, however, we were taken under very heavy fire, and things began to happen in a hurry. Our attack was in open wedge formation on a front of about a thousand yards. On my right was the first platoon commanded by Lt. Schlicht Billy. He was a Choctaw Indian from Oklahoma, and had been commissioned on the battlefield and was a courageous and resourceful fighting man in whom I had the utmost confidence. … Opposite us in the Siegfried fortifications was a seasoned Nazi division, backed up by the 29th Panzer Division. These were tough troops who knew all the tricks; it soon became apparent that we weren't going to push them around any!

In two hours of attacking we took heavy casualties—30, 40 men either killed or wounded, which will give you some idea. Then, all at once, Schlicht Billy scored, but he found he had a tiger by the tail!

"I'm in this pillbox and I can't get out!"

That was his message to me via radio and his position was indeed difficult. What had happened was this. Finding his platoon unable to advance in conventional fashion, Billy had taken three or four men and started crawling Indian style. They'd been successful in reaching a pillbox, killing four Germans, and getting inside the fortification. They'd been observed, however, from flanking pillboxes and now they were immobilized inside. Every time they tried to get out they were thrown back by a hail of German machine gun and rifle fire. "I can't get out," repeated Billy on the radio, "and I can't get the rest of my platoon up!" "Stay where you are! I ordered, "I'll try to get to you!"

Whatever the hazard, whatever the cost, Billy must be maintained in his position and strengthened. It was our foot in the door of the Siegfried Line, and it must be kept there. ... Taking command I ordered the men forward up the draw Billy had used to get close to the pillbox. The distance was about 1,000 yards. We lost ten men killed, half as many wounded, but we finally made it and joined Billy in the three-room pillbox.

In the attempt to extricate themselves during the night, Lieutenant Billy was wounded and had to be evacuated. Ultimately, Major Treadwell and his few troopers managed to force the surrender of the German defenders of that small section of the Siegfried Line and opened the door to a full-scale breakthrough. However, if it had not been for Lieutenant Billy's actions in seizing the first pillbox, things may not have gone as well as they did.[41]

Lieutenant Billy was later seriously wounded by shrapnel, which caused him to be evacuated to the United States. He was awarded the Silver Star with oak leaf cluster, five Bronze Stars, the Purple Heart, the European-African-Middle Eastern Campaign Medal, the American Defense Medal, and the good Conduct Medal.[42]

In November 1989, the French Government bestowed the Chevalier de L'Ordre National du Merite (Knight of the Order of National Merit) posthumously to the Choctaw code talkers of World War I and World War II and the Comanche code talkers of World War II.[43]

Chevalier de L'Ordre National du Merite.
www.seine-et-marne.gouv.fr.

Comanche

Listed as Comanche code talkers are: Charles Chibitty, Haddon Codynah, Robert Holder, Forrest Kassanavoid, Wellington Mihecoby, Albert Jr. (or Edward) Nahquaddy, Perry Noyabad, Clifford Otitivo, Simmons Parker, Melvin Permansu, Elgin Red Elk, Roderick Red Elk, Larry Saupitty, Anthony Tabbytite, Morris Tabbyetchy, Ralph Wahnee, Morris Sunrise, and Willis Yacheschi.

Comanche Code Talkers at Fort Benning, Georgia, 194. 1. Front row, left to right: Roderick Red Elk, Simmons Parker, Larry Saupitty, Melvin Permansu, Willie Yackeschi, Charles Chibitty, and Wellington Mihecoby. Back row, left to right: Morris Sunrise, Perry Noyabad, Ralph Wahnee, Haddon Codynah, Robert Holder, Edward Nahquaddy, Clifford Otitivo, and Forrest Kassanavoid. paulandert.com.

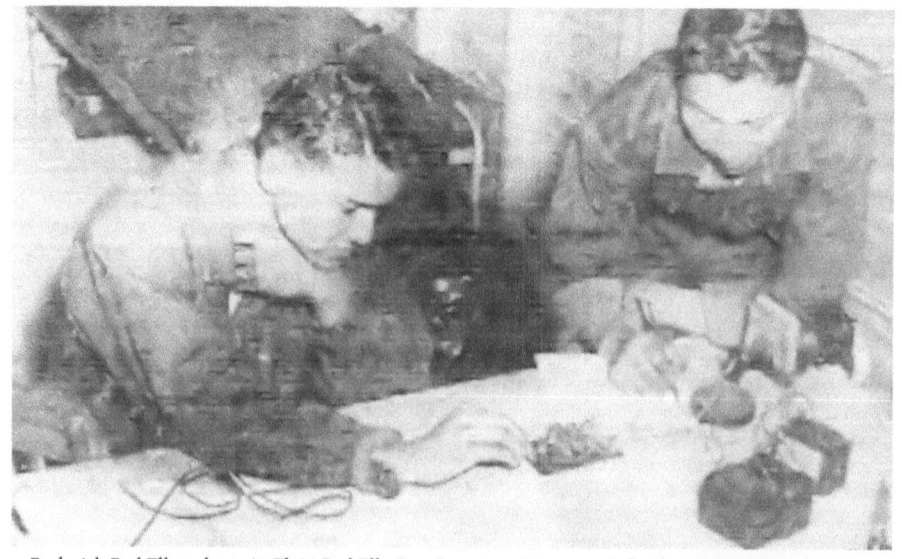

Roderick Red Elk and cousin Elgin Red Elk, Fort Benning, GA, 1941. *Columbus (GA) Ledger-Enquirer.*

Comanche were recruited for the Signal Corps from December 1940 to January 1941. An article entitled, "Under the Indian Sign," was published before the Comanche were actively recruited, stating the War Department requested thirty Comanche be recommended for the Signal Corps and undergo training in Atlanta, Georgia, as telephone operators. "Telephone operators" were also mentioned in a 13 December 1940 article in *The New York Times*:

> Oklahoma's Comanche Indians, whose strange tongue not more than thirty white men in the world can fathom, will be ready again to defy decoders as they did in the World War.

> Professor W. G. Becker of the English Department at Cameron Agricultural College, Lawton [Oklahoma], and an authority on the tribe, recalled that several Comanche from Southwestern Oklahoma were used for relaying secret messages in the last way, and added, "One would be at a telephone at the front in communication with another back at headquarters. They would relay order in their native language. The Germans had tapped the wires, and it must have driven them crazy."[44]

Simmons Parker, left, and Charles Chibitty in "Fancy Feather" dancing attire with comrades of the 6th Army Signal Company at Fort Benning Georgia. National Archives photograph.

Contrary to popular belief, the Marines, acting upon the suggestion of Philip Johnston, were not the first to establish a code talker program with the Navajo. Rather, Johnston got the idea of using Native Americans as code talkers from a newspaper article dealing with an armored division on practice maneuvers in Louisiana. During those operations, officers of the Army tried to form a secret method of communicating using their Indian troops. The Comanche who took part in the IV Corps Maneuvers in August 1941 at Dry Prong, Louisiana, returned to Fort Benning on 27 August where they began formatting their own code. This was some sixteen months before the Marine Corps began its program with the Navajo. The Comanche unit, assigned to the 4th Signal Company, 4th Infantry Division, finished its code development and used it in the 1st Army Carolina Maneuvers, Fort Jackson, South Carolina, November–December 1941, and in the Carolina Maneuvers in July 1942. The first Navajo platoon of code talkers did not finish its training until summer 1942.[45]

Haddon Codynah described how he became a code talker:

> Well when I was a senior in high school at Haskell Indian School at Lawrence, Kansas, I came home for Christmas vacation of 1940. And when I got there I was around visiting my friend and that's when my cousin across the road told me he was going, Larry Saupitty, my aunt's boy. And later I heard the other boys that I go to school with at was going … .They [the Army] were going to make a special unit of

In the barracks, Fort-Benning. Front row, l-r, Charles Chibitty, Robert Holder, Haddon Codynah, Willie Yackeschi, Elgin Red Elk, and Simmons Parker. Back row, l-r, Roderick Red Elk, Clifton Ottitvo, Wellington Mihecoby, and Morris Sunrise. *Columbus (GA) Ledger-Enquirer.*

Comanches that could speak the tribe (tribal language) fluently. So since my kin folks was going, I said, "I might as well go with them." … So that's when I went with the guys to Oklahoma City and we all joined up.⁴⁶

Albert Nahquaddy, Jr., who was related to eleven of the other sixteen who would be trained as code talkers stated when he learned of their decision to join, he did not want to be left behind, so decided to join, too.

Roderick Red Elk was among the seventeen Comanche selected for communications training prior to World War II. His reason for joining the Army was, "I knew all the people that they were recruiting. It would be just like home … . See, I knew all of them so that would be an enticement to go into a branch of service where you know a bunch of them."⁴⁷ When he and the others got to Fort Benning, sixteen of the seventeen were products of Indian boarding schools where they learned the military routine. When they first were taken to the drill field, their sergeant gave them marching commands. All but the one who hadn't gone to a boarding school performed with the precision as trained soldiers, "like we'd been in the Army all our lives." He was stunned and asked us if we were sure we were raw recruits. They answered, Yeah. "We just got in. So he dismissed us."⁴⁸

Charles Joyce Chibitty was a student at the Haskell Indian School in Lawrence, Kansas, when his parents granted him permission to enlist in the United States Army on 26 December 1941. Chibitty served in the 6th Army Signal Company in the 4th Infantry Division, and survived the Battle of Normandy. He earned the World War II Victory Medal, the European Theater of Operations Victory Medal with five Bronze Stars, the European-African-Middle Eastern Campaign Medal and the Good Conduct Medal plus the Combat Infantryman Badge.

The following brief account of the Comanche code talkers in World War II, appeared in, "Untold Stories: Rediscovering the U.S. Army's Code Talkers," *Soldiers: The Official U.S. Army Magazine:*

> Like the Choctaw in World War I, the Comanche codes included descriptive terms for military technology, such as *tutsahkuna' tawo'i'* (sewing machine gun) for machine gun; *wakaree'e* (turtle) for tank; and *Po'sa taiboo'* (crazy white man) for Adolf Hitler. The Comanche eventually encoded about 250 different military terms, and to further confuse the Germans, later created their own alphabet to spell out names and places. (Comanche had never been written down and so lacked an alphabet.) For example, they used *saddi*, Comanche for dog, to represent the English letter D. "To encrypt messages by machines and send them and decode them … sometimes

Charles Joyce Chibitty (1921–2005) served in the 6th Army Signal Company in the 4th Infantry Division, and survived the Battle of Normandy. Chibitty participated in fighting at St. Lo, Hurtgen Forest, the Battle of the Bulge, and the rescue of the "lost battalion." He earned the World War II Victory Medal, the European Theater of Operations Victory Medal with five Bronze Stars, the European-African-Middle Eastern Campaign Medal, and the Good Conduct Medal. Also Combat Infantryman Badge. In 1999, he received a Knowlton Award from the Military Intelligence Corps Association at the Pentagon's Hall of Heroes. www.dday-overlord.com/forum/des-indiens-comanches-ayant-debarque-utah-beach-bientot-commemores-t8119.html.

took, depending on the length of the message, two to four and a half hours to do this," ... "The code talker could get on the phone and it's as fast as I talking to you. ... Even if people are listening to us, we're not worrying about it."

The Comanche, who served with the 4th Signal Company, 4th Infantry Division, are the best known Army code talkers. Thirteen landed on Utah Beach in Normandy, France, on D-Day, June 6, 1944, and the following day. Wahahrockah-Tasi, a distant niece of two of the code talkers—Cpl. Charles Chibitty and Pfc. Larry Saupitty—said that many of the soldiers were related and enlisted together. Chibitty and Saupitty, for example, were first cousins.

Chibitty, who was considered the last Comanche code talker when he died in 2005, told the American Forces Press Service in 2002 he had been to Indian boarding school in the 1920s, where he was punished if he was "caught talking Indian. I told my cousin (Saupitty) that they're trying to make little white boys of us." He found his new job rather ironic: "Now they want us to talk Indian."

All but one of the Comanche code talkers had attended Fort Sill Indian School in Lawton, Oklahoma, which did have one advantage, according to Wahahrockah-Tasi, "It taught them how to march. In fact, they could begin creating their own code and training with radios and signals and Morse code much faster than normal because boarding school had already taught them fundamental military skills." One of her favorite family stories actually involves training. "Their sergeant dropped them off at a beach and told them they needed to learn how to swim," she said. "When he came back, they were swimming very well, actually floating on their backs having a good old, merry time. So when they got out

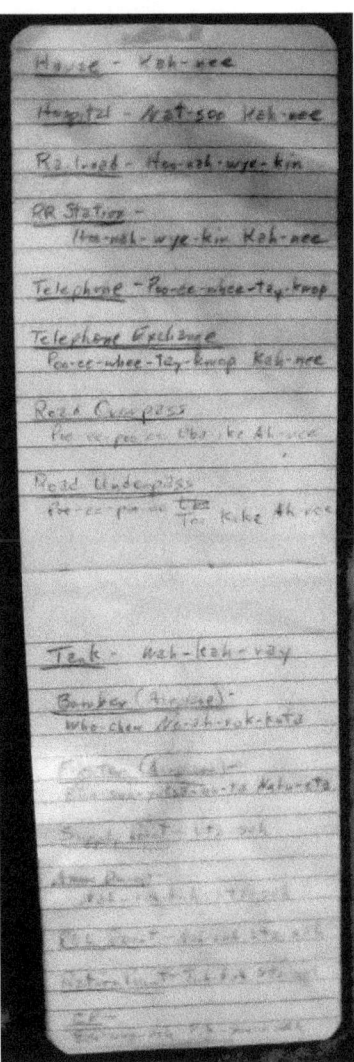

Page from a Comanche codebook.
Comanche National Museum and Cultural Center, Lawton, OK.

of the water, he said, 'You guys learned to swim fast.' One of the code talkers, Larry, told him, 'You never asked if we already knew how to swim.'"

Those swimming skills became important during the D-Day landings. The 4th Infantry Division had been tasked with meeting 82d and 101st Airborne soldiers who had parachuted into Normandy the night before, but elements of the division landed about 2,000 yards south of the designated landing point. Brig. Gen. Theodore Roosevelt Jr., turned to Pfc. Larry Saupitty, who happened to be his driver and orderly, and ordered him to report they had arrived, albeit at the wrong location. He didn't want the Germans to figure out where they were, so the message was delivered in Comanche language, "Tsaaku nunnuwee. Atahtu nunnuwee," which translates to: "We made a good landing. We landed in the wrong place."[49]

As the day wore on, the 4th Infantry Division encountered stiffer resistance on Utah Beach, which is reflected in one of Chibitty's messages: "Five miles to the right of the designated area and five miles inland, the fighting is fierce and we need help." After landing and while under heavy fire, the Comanche, as signal soldiers, then had to string wires on the beachhead.[50]

According to Meadows, Comanche code talkers served in France, Luxembourg, Belgium, and Germany, including the liberation of Paris and the Battles

Comanche code talkers in Normandy, June 1944. www.dailymail.co.uk.

of St. Lo, Hurtgen Forest, and Bastogne. They survived the Battle of the Bulge and helped assault the Siegfried Line. For example, another message Chibitty remembered sending was: "A turtle is coming down the hedgerow. Get that stovepipe and shoot him." This meant an enemy tank was coming and the unit on the other end of the line should prepare to shoot him with a bazooka.

Despite high casualty rates in the 4th Infantry Division, the Comanche code talkers, who were scattered in two-man teams throughout the division, all survived the war, although several were wounded. Saupitty was actually hit by two different shells and seriously wounded in the head, lung, and arm shortly after D-day in the fierce French hedgerow battles. After his unit found him an hour and a half later, he was sent back to England to recover and was unable to return to his unit until shortly before war's end. According to Wahahrock-ah-Tasi, Saupitty even wrote down the place he was wounded on a Nazi flag he acquired.[51] Saupitty's brother Floyd served as a U.S. Marine in World War II.[52]

Charles Chibitty was presented with the Knowlton Award in recognition of his significant contributions to military intelligence efforts. In 1989, the French Government honored the Comanche Code Talkers by presenting them the "Chevalier of the National Order of Merit." In 1992, former Secretary of Defense Dick Cheney presented Charlie with a certificate of appreciation for his service to the country. Chibitty has also received a special proclamation from the Governor of Oklahoma who honored him for his contribution both to Oklahoma and the United States.[53] In a 2004 interview at the National Museum of the American Indian, Chibitty spoke of the Normandy landings, "Utah Beach in Normandy was something else. Everybody asked me if I would go through it again, and I said no, but I could train the younger ones how we used our language and let them go ahead and do it because it was hell."

Fourteen of the Comanche Code Talkers were sent overseas during World War II to fight in the European Theater. Thirteen of those men hit the beaches of Normandy with Allied troops on D-day.

Roderick Red Elk also landed with the 4th Infantry Division at Utah Beach on D-day. In a September 1992 interview with Gary Robinson, author of, *The Language of Victory*, Red Elk, after relating his entry into the Army, his training at Fort Benning in January 1941, and how he and his fellow Comanche got together and decided upon what words or phrases could be used for military terms in their own language, told a story of his first day and night in France:

> ... As you know after we hit the beach we just—wherever the infantry hit resistance we would stop and we would clear the resistance, and then we would go. And we did that the first day from six o'clock in the morning until dark. So we pulled into this little—there

in France they call hedgerows. ... So we pulled into this placed, and just as we pulled in, I said, "We are going to spend the night.... And man, I scrambled for the nearest hedgerow and luckily there was already a foxhole dug there. ... So I take my helmet off and I laid my gun across my belly and laid flat on my back and went to sleep. I wake up in the morning in good daylight, I look on the other side on the foxhole and there sits a German soldier with his rifle lying across his lap—his eyes wide open. And I just froze, I didn't know what to do, I thought well, one of us has got to make a move. So, I grabbed my gun and swung it over to him and he never moved. So I go over there to check him and sure enough—I slept with a dead enemy all night long and didn't know it. ... I just showed the dead German how fast I could get out of the hole.[54]

Another Comanche code talker interviewed by Robinson was Forrest Kassanavoid. He decided to join the Army when he graduated from high school and could not find a job. Several of his friends joined the infantry and went to Fort Sam Houston, Texas. "I was hoping to go with them, but when I heard they were recruiting Comanche for the Signal Corps, I thought I'd try this instead—we went to Fort Benning, Georgia."[55] When speaking with Robinson, he also recalled a humorous incident. His fellow Comanche code talker, Perry Noyabad, decided not to dig a foxhole one night and laid down on the ground to sleep. A few hours later German bombers raided the area, dropping butterfly bombs. Noyabad had no foxhole to take cover in, so he jumped into a garbage pit. Unfortunately, the pit has filled with tin cans and he cut his feet up pretty badly. After the bombers passed, Noyabad went to the aid station to be treated. After bandaging his wounds, Kassanavoid remembered what his friend said when the medics tried to pin a Purple Heart on him (he already had several). He said he didn't want a Purple Heart for jumping into a garbage pit.

Robinson also interviewed Charles Chibbity, who told a story that topped those related by Red Elk and Kassanavoid.

My older brother (Bobby) was in Normandy same time I was. The next time I met him, he came in from southern Germany, and his division moved next to mine. Me and him got together and we were sitting there and he says, "Where can I get hold of one of you (code talkers)?" ... "Let me have that telephone." So, I got hold of one boy named Yekeshak [Willis Yacheschi]—he was with the 8th Infantry Regiment. And my brother told him (jokingly and in Comanche), "I am your enemy." And then he said, I understand your Comanche language." He said (Chibbity says the sentence in Comanche), "Go ahead and talk. I'll write it down." ... And Yekeshak was one of us code talkers. He said, "Who are you?" And my brother said again, "I am your enemy." And Bobby said, I am (really) Charles' brother. My division moved close to yours and I am just talking to you.: My brother got a big kick out of that.[56]

Whether Yacheschi saw the humor in it is doubtful.

Bessie Wahnee, the widow of Pfc. Ralph Wahnee, said her husband never once mentioned the war. They had actually been in touch on and off throughout World War II, finally marrying in 1945, years after they met at a dance hall outside the then-Camp Gordon, Georgia., when she was just 14. She knew most of his friends from the war, but none of them ever talked about their service either, or if they did, they didn't talk about it in English. They always just had a good time. Her husband didn't even open up when he got a letter from the French government that said it wanted to honor the code talkers.[57]

Comanche Nation Code Talkers Medal. The obverse design (left) features the Comanche Code and Spirit Talker Monument located at Comanche Nation headquarters. Inscriptions are COMANCHE CODE TALKERS and NUMUNU, Comanche language for "people." The reverse design (right) features the Comanche Nation logo, the 90th Infantry Division insignia on the left and the 4th Infantry Division insignia on the right. Inscriptions are PUHIHWITEKWA EKASAHPANA, WORLD WAR I, WORLD WAR II and ACT OF CONGRESS 2008. According to the Comanche Nation, when loosely interpreted, puhihwitekwa ekasahpana means "soldiers talking on phones made of metal." http://www.usmint.gov/mint_programs/medals/?action=codeTalkers.

Crow Nation

Barney Old Coyote, Jr., Henry Old Coyote, Samson Birdinground, and Cyril Not Afraid.

Gail Schontzler, *Chronicle* Staff Writer wrote of Barney Old Coyote in the 27 November 2011 issue of the *Bozeman Daily Chronicle*:

> Barney Old Coyote, Jr., became the most decorated American Indian in World War II. He was seventeen when the Japanese attacked Pearl Harbor on 7 December 1941. The next day, Barney and four other boys from Hardin High School took the bus to Billings, Montana, to join the Army. But Barney was a minor, and his adoptive parents refused to sign the enlistment papers. "We wanted a child," they said, "not a gold star in the window." "My natural father said, 'I'll sign for you, keep you with the warrior tradition. You're seventeen, you can go to war like we always did,'" Barney recalled. So he enlisted under his original name, Barney Old Coyote Jr. His brother Henry, nine years older, promised to look out for him. His mother sent a letter to the secretary of war, asking that Barney and Henry not be separated, despite Army policy. The secretary of the Army sent a letter saying that they would make every effort to keep the brothers together. The brothers trained as airplane mechanics in Long Beach, California, and went to gunnery school in Panama City, Florida, with movie star Clark Gable. Just before shipping out to England in 1942, the brothers participated in a Sun Dance ceremony at Crow Agency.
>
> His World War II military career was marked by high distinctions that he shared with his brother Henry. Barney was listed in *Stars and Stripes* magazine as a recipient on the Soldiers Medal. His military record consists of combat and noncombat medals including the Air Medal with oak clusters, the Silver Star with cluster, campaign medals with several battle stars. Barney and Henry fought side-by-side as

Barney Old Coyote. www.billingsgazette.com.

Boeing B-17 Flying Fortress gunners for more than fifty missions over Belgium, Germany, and France during World War II. As part of their service, they used the Crow language to break radio silence and get messages past the German code breakers. Barney would later write about his World War II experiences with Henry in "My Brother My Buddy." In the excerpt, Barney wrote about a bombing run where he and Henry led two waves of planes respectively, 144 total, in a high-level bombing of France. During the attack run, they spoke in Crow over the radio. Five hundred enemy planes were destroyed. In all, they flew fifty missions aboard the B-24 bomber called the "Exterminator." In 1964, Barney was appointed as a special assistant to the secretary of the interior under President Lyndon B. Johnson.[58]

Crow Nation Code Talkers Medal. The obverse design (left) depicts a variation of the Army Air Corps Wings and is inscribed CROW CODE TALKERS. The reverse design (right) features the Crow Nation Seal. Inscriptions are WORLD WAR II and ACT OF CONGRESS 2008. www.usmint.gov/mint_programs/medals/?action=codeTalkers.

Fond-du-Lac-Band-of-Lake-Superior Chippewa Tribe

Although Lex C. Porter is listed as the only member of his tribe who served as a code talker in World War II. However, if Porter was engaged in befuddling the enemy, there certainly was another as yet unidentified member of the tribe at the other end of the line. In fact Meadows reports, "In the autumn of 1940, seventeen Oneida and Chippewa from Michigan and Wisconsin joined the 32d Infantry Regiment for the specific purpose of receiving training in adapting their native languages for radio communication. Nine men from western Wisconsin were with the provisional antitank battalion; four from Northern Wisconsin were with the 57th Field Artillery Brigade; and four from northern Michigan were assigned to the division command."[59] Lex's grandson, Freedom Porter, said the family knew that Lex had served in the Army during World War II. They knew that he was one of many Native American men who enlisted on 8 December 1941, the day after the horrific attack on Pearl Harbor. Freedom Porter remembers his grandmother telling him that most of the men from Grand Portage left that day, heading to Fort Snelling to enlist (the official date of his enlistment was 17 January 1942). He served in the Pacific Theater.[60]

Fond du Lac Band of Lake Superior Chippewa Tribe Code Talkers Medal. The obverse design (left) depicts a World War II code talker transcribing and receiving information. A beading pattern is at the bottom rim of the design and foliage is incorporated at the top rim, representing the Fond du Lac Tribe code talkers who served in the South Pacific. Inscriptions are "LAKE SUPERIOR BAND OF FOND DU LAC CHIPPEWA" and "CODE TALKERS." The reverse design (right) features the Fond du Lac Band of Lake Superior Chippewa Tribe Seal. Inscriptions are "ACT OF CONGRESS 2008," "WORLD WAR II," "FOND DU LAC" and BAPASHKOMINITIGONG OGITCHIDAAG, which translates to "Fond du Lac soldiers" or "Fond du Lac warriors." www.usmint.gov/mint_programs/medals/?action=codeTalkers.

Hopi

Ten Hopi developed a code language, which they used to assist U.S. Army intelligence in the Marshall Islands, New Caledonia, and the Philippines during World War II: Franklin Shupla, Warren Koiyaquaptewa, Frank Chapella, Travis Yaiva, Charles Lomakema, Percival Navenma, Perry Honani, Sr., Floyd Dann, Sr., in the Army, 81st Infantry "Wildcat" Division during the Peleliu, Angaur, and Philippine campaigns as well as several others. They were specifically assigned to the 321st, 322d and 323d Regiments of the 81st, and Rex Pooyouma and Orville Wadsworth who served in the 380th Bombardment Group (Flying Circus), 5th Army Air Corps.

These soldiers served in the Pacific. They went ashore toward the end of the Guadalcanal fighting, but not as code talkers, although they may have communicated with each other in their native language. They returned to the United States in 1943 and underwent training in Arizona. Franklin Shupla, one of their number, stated group members "went to extraordinary lengths to use Hopi words and concepts to come up with terms for battle." The Hopi first used their language during the campaign for the Marshall Islands and later during the battle for New Caledonia. They were subsequently sent to the Philippines. Their language allowed them to make jokes about their commanders, without fear of getting caught.[61]

Cpl. Orville Wadsworth. 380th Bomb Group Association, www.380th.org.

Pvt. Floyd Dann talking to other members of his tribe on maneuvers with the Second Army. www.azcentral.com.

Sgt. Rex Pooyouma, 380th Bomb Group Association,
www.380th.org.

Hopi Tribe Code Talkers Medal (facing page). The obverse design (left) features Hopi code talkers communicating on a field phone and using binoculars to search for the enemy. The B-24 Liberator in the background represents the Hopi code talkers' service in the 90th and 380th Bombardment Groups. Inscriptions are HOPI CODE TALKERS and U.S. ARMY. The reverse design (right) features a variation of the Hopi Tribe flag, which depicts a circle with dots, mountains and stalks of corn on both sides of the mountains. The flag's symbols represent the Hopi way of life. Inscriptions are WORLD WAR II, ACT OF CONGRESS 2008, A CODE NEVER BROKEN, KEPT AMERICA FREE and HOPILAVAYI, which in English means "Hopi language." www.usmint.gov/mint_programs/medals/?action=codeTalkers.

Kiowa

Kiowa Code Talkers of World War II: Leonard Cozad Sr., John Tsatoke, and Jim Paddlety, all who served in the 689th Field Artillery Battalion, XX Corps.

Kiowa Tribe Code Talkers Medal. The obverse design (left) depicts a code talker using a field phone to communicate. Inscriptions are KIOWA TRIBE CODE TALKERS and 689TH FIELD ARTILLERY, EUROPE, the U.S. Army unit in which the Kiowa Tribe members served. The reverse design (right) depicts the Kiowa Tribe logo. Inscriptions are DEDICATION, HONOR, VALOR, WORLD WAR II and ACT OF CONGRESS 2008. www.usmint.gov/mint_programs/medals/?action=codeTalkers.

Menominee

Dan Waupoose, John C. O'Katchekum, Mose Wausakokamick, Dave Mathapotow and William Matchapatow.

Menominee Nation Code Talkers Medal. The obverse (left) depicts a code talker using communication equipment while three P-51 Mustangs fly overhead. Inscriptions are MENOMINEE CODE TALKERS and OMAEQNOMENEW KEMOC KEKETOTATOWAK, which translates to "Menominee secretly talk to each other." The reverse (right) features the Thunderbird, which is the center element of the Menominee Nation Seal, the five clans (bear, eagle, wolf, moose, and crane), a sturgeon, and wild rice. The Menominee Nation is known for its reliance on wild rice and intense fishing, especially for sturgeon. Inscriptions are WORLD WAR II and ACT OF CONGRESS 2008. www.usmint.gov/mint_programs/medals/?action=codeTalkers.

Dan Waupose, a Menominee chief, training at Algiers, LA, 24. August 1943. www.warhistoryonline.com.

Meskwaki (Sac and Fox)

Eight members of the Meskwaki Tribe, originally members of the 18th Iowa Infantry were selected for special instruction in the use of the walkie-talkies, communications radios, and machine guns, served as code talkers in the 168th Infantry Regiment, 34th Division in North Africa. Frank Sanache was a code talker, ventured out far beyond the battalion and used a walkie-talkie to direct artillery fire in the desert, ... "It was the worst place this side of hell," said Sanache. Sanache was one of twenty-seven Meskwaki, then sixteen percent of Iowa's male Meskwaki population, to enlist in the Iowa National Guard together in January 1941, nearly a year before Pearl Harbor. Eight of the group—Sanache, his brother Willard, Dewey Young Bear, Edward Benson, Judie Wayne Wabaunasee, Mike Wayne Wabaunasee, Dewey Roberts and Malvin "Mike" Twain—became code talkers. The challenge during this experimental phase was to take the Native language and cross-reference Meskwaki words with military terms that were not in the Native language. A "colonel" was a "silver eagle," a "fighter plane" became "hummingbird," "minesweeper" became "beaver," "half-track" became "race track," a "tank" was a 'turtle, 'and "pyrotechnic" became "fancy fire." The Meskwaki men trained at Marshalltown and Camp Dodge, Iowa, but they were soon sent to Camp Claiborne, Louisiana, for jungle warfare training. They served together in Company H, the heavy weapons company of the 168th Infantry, 34th "Red Bull" Division. After completing their training in Louisiana and code talker training in Scotland and England, they were sent to North Africa. Sanache told how he would be sent out as a scout. ... They used to send him about two miles ahead of the troops in dangerous conditions. There were only eight of them so they worked 24-hour shifts. "The walkie-talkies squealed and chattered so loudly, it was difficult to hear one another," said Don Wanatee, Sanache's adopted grandson. "There simply weren't enough of them to effectively transmit messages between the eight companies in the division."

Meskwaki code talker Pvt. Dewey Young Bear adjusting the radio backpack carried by Pvt. Willard Sanache, another of his group. www.msswarriors.org.

Sanache was captured by Italian soldiers in Tunisia in 1943. Dewey Youngbear and Judy Wayne Wabaunasee were captured by the Germans. Sanache was sent to a camp in Hammerstein, Poland, where he was held until the Allies liberated the camp at the end of the war. For twenty-nine months, his days were spent unloading lime from rail cars, leaving him with scarred lungs and

Meskwaki code talkers, 1941. www.soldiers.dodlive.mil.

a variety of chronic illnesses. His daily rations included a cup of soup, two boiled potatoes, a glass of water and a slice of bread.[62] Besides suffering harsh treatment, American Indians, rarely seen in Europe, faced racial prejudice in Italian and German POW camps. The Meskwaki, like other POWs, had to learn the German language fairly quickly, for if they didn't respond to a command, they would be beaten. Donald Wanatee, said, "They didn't treat them well. They worked them to death."[63] The desperate feelings of these men lead to numerous escape attempts. Dewey Youngbear, who no doubt paid a heavy price each time he was recaptured. On his third attempt, he managed to find an Italian soldier's uniform to wear as a disguise but was identified because he didn't know the language. Judy Wayne Wabaunasee also escaped his captors in Italy but later, when he arrived at the same prison camp in Germany, guards noticed that Youngbear and Wabaunasee knew each other. They both received "rough treatment" for refusing to give information about the other.

As with many POWs, they required hospitalization after their release, and they suffered life-long problems. Youngbear died in 1948 of tuberculosis he contracted as a POW. Other Meskwaki veterans also had war-related health problems.[64]

U.S. Army Native American Code Talkers in World Wars I and II 61

"Original Americans." Eight Meskwaki code talkers: L-r, Mike Wayne Wabaunasee, Edward Benson, Dewey Roberts, Frank Senache, Judie Wayne Wabaunasee (reclining), Malvin Twain (rear, stting). Standing, rear, Willard Senache and Dewey Young Bear. www.msswarriors.org.

Meskwaki Nation Code Talkers Medal. The obverse design (left) features two code talkers in action. Inscriptions are MESKWAKI NATION CODE TALKERS and ne me skwa, ki i be na, which translates to "We are the red earth people." The reverse design (right) features a variation of the Meskwaki Nation logo. Inscriptions are ACT OF CONGRESS 2008, WORLD WAR I and WORLD WAR II. www.usmint.gov/mint_programs/medals/?action=codeTalkers.

Akwesasne Mohawk

Pvt. Joe King, Pfc. Alex W. Lazore, Joe Harry Pike, Pfc. Angus B. Cook, Pvt. Mike Arquette, Pfc. Joseph Barnes, Pvt. Thomas Cole, Angus J. Laughing, Pvt. Alex Oakes, 82d Airborne Division, Pvt. Mitchell P. Sunday, Pvt. Albert Tarbell, 82d Airborne Division, Pfc. Reginald White, Louis L. Oakes, T/5, Company B, 442d Signal Battalion, Louis Stanley Connors, Pfc. Louis E. King, Alex W. Peters, and Charles Lazore, 101st Airborne Division.

Top row, left to right:
Pvt. Joe King; Pfc. Alex Wilson Lazore, 75th Artillery; Pfc. Angus B Cook; Joe Harry Pike; Mike Arquette.

Middle row, left to right:
Pfc. Joseph Barnes; Pvt. Thomas Cole; Angus J. Laughing; Pfc. Alex Oakes 82d Airborne; Pfc. Mitchell Sunday.

Bottom row, left to right:
Pfc. Reginald White; Louis Stanley Conners; Pfc. Louie S. King; Alex W. Peters; Charles Lazore, 101st Airborne. "Program for the Congressional Medal Ceremony honoring Akwesasne Mohawk Code Talkers, Akwesasne, NY, 28 May 2016."

In a 2016 interview, Pvt. Louis L. Oakes, the last surviving Akwesasne Mohawk code talker of WW II, recalled, "There were only three or four other code talkers in Company B," but laughed when he was asked if he could remember how many secret messages he relayed in the Mohawk tongue. "If I can't talk it out, I'll give them a smoke signal," Oakes said. "We talked about field wires in the jungles. They would give you a piece of paper to read on telling you what you were to say." "And you did it OK?" someone yelled to him over the sound of the crowd.

"Oh yeah, I'm still here," Oakes said with a grin.

T/4 Louis Levi Oakes, Co. B, 4. 4. 2d Signal Battalion. "Program for the Congressional Medal Ceremony honoring Akwesasne Mohawk Code Talkers, Akwesasne, NY, 28 May 2016."

But unlike Oakes, Albert A. Tarbell was filled with stories, according to his son, Mitchell "Mike" Tarbell. Albert Tarbell was the first Mohawk in the 82nd Airborne Division during WW II, serving in the 504th Parachute Infantry Regiment. He died in 2009, a day after his 86th birthday, Mike Tarbell said,

> He went right through North Africa to Anzio Beachhead, [and later] jumped into Holland during Operation Market Garden. He went all the way through [the war] right up to the Battle of the Bulge, to the Elbe River to meet the Russians and then he became a Berlin Honor Guard. So that was the end of the war and they were basically making it safe." Tarbell said because his father was in communications, his job included taking care of communications wiring on the battlefield. There was one story about a job his father had, during the Battle of the Bulge that stayed with him most. "He had volunteered to go out and take care of some bad wiring because they couldn't get the field lines working and where he had to go was between the Germans and the Americans, my dad's own guys," Tarbell said, a smile growing on his face from the memory. "What he found out was that as he was following the lead line, he was going by these houses and so he kept following out and he prepared the wire and he came back by this house." Nearly fifty years later, during a reunion for the battle, he said his father was retelling the story when a former German officer let

Albert Tarbell, 82d Airborne. "Program for the Congressional Medal Ceremony honoring Akwesasne Mohawk Code Talkers, Akwesasne, NY, 28 May 2016."

him know just how much danger he was in. The German told him he was hiding in one of those houses with his squad and was deciding whether he was going to shoot him. "He said, 'if we had shot you that would have given away our position and our counterattack wouldn't have worked,' so my dad had a chance," Tarbell said. "And there are a lot of stories like that."[65]

Akwesasne Mohawk Code Talkers Medal. The obverse design (left) features a World War II code talker, a snipe, and the principal clans of the Mohawk Tribe—a bear, a wolf, and a snapping turtle. It is inscribed with AKWESASNE MOHAWK CODE TALKERS. The reverse design (right) features a profiled figure, a Mohawk kustowa headdress, a bear claw necklace, a war club, and a Mohawk Wolf Belt. Inscriptions are WORLD WAR I, WORLD WAR II, and ACT OF CONGRESS 2008. www.usmint.gov/mint_programs/medals/?action=codeTalkers.

Muscogee Creek Nation

Leslie Richards and Thomas McIntosh.

Muscogee Creek Nation Code Talkers Medal. The obverse design (left) features a code talker speaking on his field phone. The inscription is MUSCOGEE CREEK NATION CODE TALKERS. The reverse design (right) depicts lacrosse sticks and a ball. Inscriptions are WORLD WAR II and ACT OF CONGRESS 2008. www.usmint.gov/mint_programs/medals/?action=codeTalkers.

Oneida Nation

Rimton L. Doxtator, Company E, Hudson Doxtator,: Lloyd Schuyler, and Rupert S. Adams.

As a young man, Hudson Doxtater joined the United States Army and achieved the rank of corporal. During his twelve years of service he served in World War II and was in battle in New Guinea, Southern Philippines, and Luzon. He subsequently served during the Korean Conflict He served in the Service Co, 5th Cavalry Regiment. He was awarded the Philippine Liberation Medal, Asiatic-Pacific Theater Service Medal, American Theater Service Medal for World War II. He also received the Korean Service Medal with three battle stars, United Nations Medal, Good Conduct Medal and the Combat Infantry Badge.

Lloyd M. Schuyler served seventeen years in the United States Army and participated in World War II and the Korean War. He belonged to 3d Gun Section, Battery C, 985th Field Artillery. For his participation in four World War II battles and six Korean War battles Lloyd received multiple medals and recognitions including: the European African Middle Eastern Campaign Medal with four battle stars, American Defense Service Medal, Korean Service Medal with five Bronze Stars, United Nation Service Medal, Meritorious Unit Commendation, Presidential Unit Citation, the National Defense Service Medal, and the Army Occupation Medal.

Rupert S. Adams joined the Army and served for 5 years and 28 days during World War II. He served in Africa, Naples-Foggia, and Po Valley in Battery A, 527th Field Artillery Battalion.

As a serviceman Adams was awarded 1 Service Stripe, 4 Overseas Service Bars, American Defense Ribbon, American Theater Ribbon, European African-Middle Eastern Theater Ribbon, 3 Bronze Stars, Good Conduct Medal, American Defense Service Medal and World War II Victory Medal.

Rimton L. Doxtater served four years with the Army National Guard, Company E, 113th Infantry Regiment, 32d Infantry Division. He was stationed in Algiers, Africa, and Italy. Rimton was wounded and received the Purple Heart.[66]

Oneida Nation Code Talkers Medal (facing page). The obverse design (left) features an Oneida Nation code talker with eagle feathers, positioned similar to those in the Oneida Gustoweh (headdress) in the background. Inscriptions are ONEIDA NATION WARRIORS and CODE TALKERS. The reverse design (right_ features the Great White Pine Tree of Peace with four white roots atop a turtle. To the left of the tree is the foot print of a bear. To the right of the tree is the foot print of a wolf. The turtle, bear and wolf represent the clans of the Oneida Nation. Atop the tree is an eagle, vigilant over the nation and warning members of any imminent danger. The symbols near or under the turtle are a war club and six arrows bound tightly together to indicate the unified strength of the six nations of the Iroquois Confederacy. An image of the two-row wampum belt, constructed of quahog beads, is at the bottom of the design. Inscriptions are WORLD WAR II, ACT OF CONGRESS 2008 and LATIWᚼNATÉNYESHSE, which translates to "They change their words." http://www.usmint.gov/mint_programs/medals/?action=codeTalkers.

Osage Nation

No member of the Osage Nation who served in World War II has been identified.

Osage Nation Code Talkers Medal. The obverse design (left) depicts a code talker looking up and focusing on his task. The barbed wire is symbolic of the threat to the soldier. Inscriptions are OSAGE NATION and CODE TALKERS. The reverse design (right) depicts a variation of the Osage Nation seal. Inscriptions are ACT OF CONGRESS 2008, WORLD WAR I and WORLD WAR II. http://www.usmint.gov/mint_programs/medals/?action=codeTalkers.

PAWNEE

Frank Davis, Brummett Echohawk, Grant Grover, Philip Grover, Enoch Jim, Harold Morgan, Floyd Rice, Henry C. Stoneroad, Jr., and Chauncey Matlock.

Seven of the nine Pawnee code talkers served with the 157th, 179th, and 180th Infantry Regiments of Oklahoma's 45th Infantry Division in the European-African-Middle Eastern Theater of Operations during World War II. They include: SSgt. Frank Davis; Sgt. Brummett Echohawk; Sgt. Grant Gover (KIA); SSgt. Phillip Gover; SSgt. Chauncey F. Matlock; Sgt. Harold W. Morgan; and MSgt. Floyd E. Rice. Sgt. Grant Gover was killed in action on 1 November 1944 during the Rhineland Campaign. The remaining six code talkers were all wounded in action, (Sergeant Echohawk three times, and Staff Sergeant Matlock twice). T/5 Henry C. Stoneroad Sr., and Sgt. Enoch Jim served in the Asiatic-Pacific Theater during World War II. Technician 5th Grade Stoneroad served with Reconnaissance Troop, 112th Regimental Combat Team, 1st Cavalry Division, and Sergeant Jim served with the 33d Infantry Division.

Sgt. Brummett Echohawk received the Bronze Star with Combat V, and three Purple Hearts. Chosen for his fighting ability and a photographic memory, he was trained as a code talker at Camp X and given the code name "Mistretta Blue."[67]

Sgt. Grant Gover was killed in action on 1 November 1944 during the Rhineland Campaign. www.okhistory.org.

Pawnee Nation Code Talkers Medal (facing page). The obverse design (left) features the full body profile of a soldier with phone and helmet in hand. It is inscribed PAWNEE NATION CODE TALKERS. The reverse design (right) depicts a variation of the Pawnee Nation seal, which includes the wolf, tomahawk, peace pipe, morning star, sage, cedar and a banner inscribed with CHATICKS-SI-CHATICKS, which translates to "men-of-men." Other inscriptions are WORLD WAR I, WORLD WAR II and ACT OF CONGRESS 2008. http://www.usmint.gov/mint_programs/medals/?action=codeTalkers.

Sgt. Brummett Echohawk. Courtesy of Mark Ellenbarger, Military Studies and Observation Group, The Brummett Echohawk Project.

Pueblo of Acoma Code Talkers Medal (facing page). The obverse design (left) features a Pueblo of Acoma code talker scouting the area during his tour of duty in the South Pacific. Inscriptions are PUEBLO OF ACOMA and CODE TALKERS. The reverse design (right) features the Pueblo of Acoma flag. Clans depicted in the flag are the antelope (at the top center); the road runner, turkey, parrot, oak and mustard seed (to the left); and an eagle, sun, bear, pumpkin, and red and yellow corn (to the right). In the center (bottom to top) are water, Abraham Lincoln's Cane of Authority presented to the tribe in 1864. , Pueblo of Acoma Sky City Village and wind. Inscriptions are WORLD WAR II and ACT OF CONGRESS 2008. http://www.usmint.gov/mint_programs/medals/?action=codeTalkers.

Ponca

William I. Snake is the only Ponca to be identified as a code talker.

Ponca Tribe Code Talkers Medal. The obverse design (left) features two code talkers in action with Chief White Eagle, a respected leader of the Ponca Tribe, in the background. It is inscribed PONCA TRIBE CODE TALKERS. The reverse design (right)features a variation of the Ponca Tribe seal, which consists of three clustered tipis with the sun behind it. Inscriptions are ACT OF CONGRESS 2008,WORLD WAR I and WORLD WAR II. www.usmint.gov/mint_programs/medals/?action=codeTalkers.

Pueblo of Acoma

One known Acoma, SSgt. Paul R. Histia, served as a code talker with the 90th Bomb Group in the South Pacific during World War II.

Seminoles

Edmond Harjo, Tony Palmer, and William Melton.

Edmond Andrew Harjo, who served with his brothers, was the last surviving code talker from the Seminole Nation of Oklahoma. He served in the U.S. Army's 195th Field Artillery Battalion. Harjo was walking through a French orchard when he heard someone singing the Mvskoke song "Yvmv Estemerketvn":

> Yvmv, estemerketvn, tehoyv nayof
> Cesvs, Vpakares

It was a religious hymn, which roughly translates as "When I Pass This Suffering."

> Here, the suffering,
> when I pass through
> I must pass through,
> I must pass through
> Jesus, I will be with.

He knew the song, and the language. He went to find who was singing.

"It was a Creek from the Muscogee area. The two men introduced themselves and began talking in Mvskoke. Then, a coincidence: an officer overheard their conversation and asked what language they were speaking. "He asked them if they'd volunteer for a new unit of code talkers," said Harjo. The story was later recounted by Speaker of the United States House of Representatives John Boehner at the Congressional Gold Medal award ceremony honoring Harjo in November 2013. He was awarded a Silver Star for his work as a code talker, as well as a European-African-Middle Eastern Campaign Medal and a Good Conduct Medal for his service during the war.

Tony Palmer joined the Army in late 1942 with two other Seminoles—William Melton of Wewoka and Edmond Harjo of Konawa. During the Southern Philippines Campaign of 1944, Maskoki speakers used their native tongue to outwit Japanese forces.[68] Palmer was awarded many medals for valor and good conduct, including the Bronze Star, Purple Heart, Good Conduct Medal and the Philippine Liberation Medal.

Pvt. Edmund Harjo in late 1944 during the Battle of the Bulge in Belgium.
www.seminolenationmuseum.org.

Cpl. Tony Palmer. www.seminolenationmuseum.org.

Seminole Nations Code Talkers Medal (facing page). The obverse design (left) features Seminole Nation code talkers with an early period chief in the background. The inscribed phrase ACEMEKET HECETV HERET OS, which translates to "It is good to climb and see," is an actual phrase used by Seminole code talkers. The other inscription is SEMINOLE CODE TALKERS. The reverse (right) design depicts a variation of the Seminole Nation of Oklahoma seal. Inscriptions are WORLD WAR II, ACT OF CONGRESS 2008 and SEMINOLE NATION OF OKLAHOMA. www.usmint.gov/mint_programs/medals/?action=codeTalkers.

Great Sioux Nation (Očhéthi Šakówiŋ)

When the Congress commemorated the Navajo code talkers in 2000, a movement began among the Sioux Nation to have its members who also served as code talkers in WW II honored.

> State of South Dakota SEVENTY-SEVENTH SESSION LEGISLATIVE ASSEMBLY, 2002 850H0803 HOUSE COMMEMORATION NO. 1026 Introduced by: Representative Gillespie and Senator Hagen A LEGISLATIVE COMMEMORATION, Honoring the Sioux Code Talkers in recognition of their great contributions and service to their nation during World War II. WHEREAS, during WW II our United States military sought a code to allow undecipherable secure communications by telephone and radio; and WHEREAS, the Sioux language, with its extreme complexity, developed into a solution for an undecipherable code; and WHEREAS, eleven American Indian Veterans from South Dakota answered the call of duty by our United States military to use their Indian languages of Dakota, Lakota, and Nakota Sioux as code language during World War II, namely: Edmund St. John of the Crow Creek Sioux Tribe, Phillip "Stoney" LaBlanc of the Cheyenne River Sioux Tribe, Baptiste Pumpkinseed of the Oglala Sioux Tribe, Eddie Eagle Boy of the Cheyenne River Sioux Tribe, Guy Rondell of the Sisseton-Whapeton Sioux Tribe, John Bear King of the Standing Rock Sioux Tribe, Iver Crow Eagle, Sr., of the Rosebud Sioux Tribe, Walter C. John of the Santee Sioux Tribe, Simon Brokenleg of the Rosebud Sioux Tribe, Clarence Wolfguts of the Oglala Sioux Tribe, and Charles Whitepipe of the Rosebud Sioux Tribe; and WHEREAS, the Sioux Code Talkers transmitted information on troop movements,

tactics, orders, and crucial intelligence; and WHEREAS, Sioux Code Talkers are credited for saving the lives of countless American and allied forces; and WHEREAS, the Sioux Code Talkers operated under some of the heaviest combat, manned radio networks, worked around the clock, and were highly successful in communications operation; and WHEREAS, these men performed an important service to the preservation of democracy and deserve recognition which is long overdue: NOW, THEREFORE, BE IT COMMEMORATED, by the Seventy-seventh Legislature of the State of South Dakota, that the South Dakota Legislature recognizes the Sioux Code Talkers and their immeasurable contribution to their nation in a great time of need.[69]

The eleven Sioux honored in this piece of legislation inspired other Sioux tribes to look into the military service of their members.

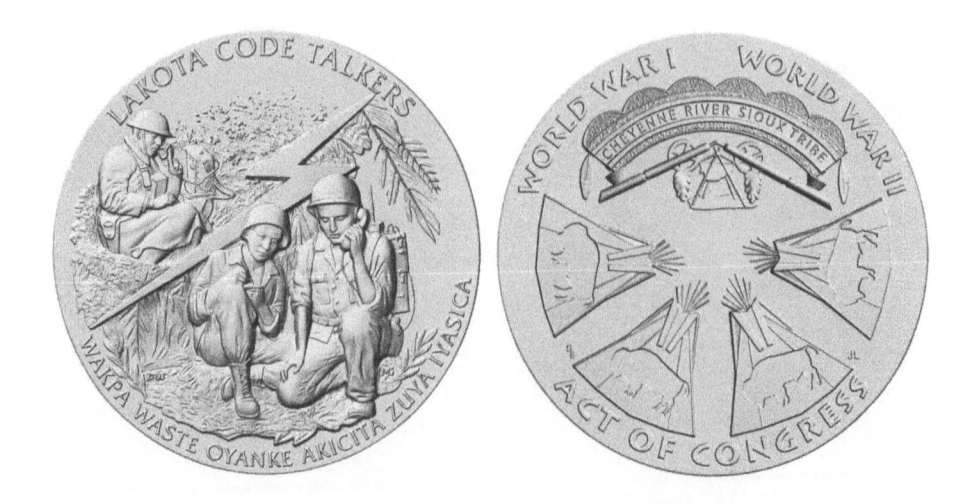

Cheyenne River Sioux

Narcisse Eagle Chasing Phillip "Stoney" LaBlanc, and Eddie Eagle Boy, are credited as code talkers, from the Cheyenne River Sioux. The *Corson County (South Dakota) News*, 17 June 1943, published the following from one of them:

> Our poetic Indian friend, Narcisse Eagle Chasing, who is somewhere in the South Pacific sends us another narrative regarding army life, in his own rollicking way:
>
>> Put this in the paper—every word is true.
>> I'm sitting here and thinking of the things I've left behind,
>> and I have put on paper what is running through my mind.
>> We've dug a million ditches and cleared ten miles of ground.
>> A meaner place this side of hell is waiting to be found.
>> But there's one small consolation, Gather closely while I tell,
>> when we die we'll go to heaven. For we've done our hitch in hell.
>>
>> We've built a hundred kitchens for the cooks to stew our beans.
>> We've stood a million guard mounts and we've never acted mean.
>> We've rolled a million blanket rolls and washed the Captain's duds.
>> We've washed a million mess kits and peeled a million spuds.
>> The number of parade's we've stood is very hard to tell.
>> But we'll not parade in heaven. For we've done our hitch in hell.
>>
>> We've killed a million bugs that have crawled from out our eats.
>> We've pulled some million centipedes from out our dirtiest sheets.
>> And we have marched a million miles and made a million camps.
>> The grub we've had to eat at times has given us the cramps.
>> But when our work on earth is done, our friends behind will tell:
>> "They surely went to heaven for they did their hitch in hell."
>>
>> When final taps is sounded and we're laid to rest
>> we will do our last parade upon those shinning golden stairs.
>> The angels all will welcome us and harps will start to play;
>> we'll draw a million canteen checks and spend them all one day.
>> The Great Commanding Officer will smile on us and say;
>> "Come, take the first seats gentlemen for you've done your bit in hell."[70]

Phillip "Stoney" LaBlanc served with the 302d Recon Squadron of the 1st Cavalry Division.

Pvt. Phillip "Stoney" LaBlanc, 302nd Recon Squadron of the 1st Cavalry Division. www.crstvets.org

Cheyenne River Sioux Tribe Code Talkers Medal (facing page). The obverse design)left) depicts a World War I soldier sitting in a trench while receiving a message over his telephone. In the lower field, a World War II soldier sits in a deciduous forest while communicating messages. Inscriptions are WAKPA WASTE OYANKE AKICITA ZUYA IYASICA, Cheyenne River Sioux language for "good river soldiers fight the enemy," and LAKOTA CODE TALKERS. The reverse design (right) features elements from the Cheyenne River Sioux flag and four tipis with buffalos imposed on them. Inscriptions are WORLD WAR I, WORLD WAR II and ACT OF CONGRESS. www.usmint.gov/mint_programs/medals/?action=codeTalkers.

Crow Creek Sioux

Edmund St. John and Joseph Reddoor.

Crow Creek Tribe Code Talkers Medal. The obverse design (left) features a World War II soldier with phone and map in hand. Inscriptions are HUNKPATI DAKOTA OYATE, CROW CREEK TRIBE and SIOUX CODE TALKERS. Hunkpati Dakota Oyate is how the tribe refers to itself. The reverse design (right) features a variation of the Crow Creek Tribe seal. Inscriptions are WORLD WAR II, and ACT OF CONGRESS 2008. www.usmint.gov/mint_programs/medals/?action=codeTalkers.

Bonnie McGhee, daughter of Edmund St. John ... recalled the moment her father revealed to her when she was a senior in high school that he was a code talker. He was recruited to be a code talker while sitting in his foxhole with another guy. A sergeant came over and pulled him out of the hole and asked him "What kind of language do you speak?"[71]

Fort Peck Assiniboine Sioux

Members of the Fort Peck Tribes acknowledged as code talkers who are identified as members of the Assiniboine Tribe are identified as Jesse Mason Jr., Charles Adams, Matt D. Adams, Joseph R. Alverez, Archie M. Cantrell, Joseph Hamilton, Adam Redd, Lawrence Red Dog, Jay H. Kirn, Duncan Dupree, John Cantrell, and Gilbert Horn, Sr.

Identified as Sioux are Anton Hollow, Joseph O. Reddoor, Herman Red Elk Jr., Clyde Standing Bear, Herman Belgarde, Arthur Belgarde, Dominick Belgarde, James J. Eder, James M. Melbourne Jr., Shirley Q. Red Boy, James Black Dog Jr., Matthew E. Black Dog, Lloyd Half Red, William Hawk, Earl Jones, Frank Jones, Ralph N. Jones, Barney Lambert, Louis E. Longee, Mark Long Tree, Raymond L. Ogle, William G. Ogle, Gerald Red Elk, William J. Red Fox, Joseph E. Russell, Gregory B. Swift Eagle, Winfield Wilson, James T. Yellow Owl, Douglas Young Man, Everett D. Bear, Richard Left Hand Thunder, Ben Little Head, Archie Red Boy, Fred R. Shields, Joseph Lambert, Harvey Buck Elk and Julian Shields.[72]

Meadows reports a "group of five Assiniboine code talkers in Company B of the 163d Infantry Regiment, 41st Infantry Division, which included James Turningbear (not listed in the U.S. Army's 'Individual Code Talkers by Tribal Affiliation') and others."[73]

In September 1940, Gilbert Horn marched with sixteen other young men through the streets of Chinook before heading to Fort Lewis for basic training. Horn's grandparents sang a warrior's song for their grandson as he marched out of town. Around his neck, Horn wore the sacred eagle plume his mother had given him for protection. He was only 15 years old.

"I was a little snotty kid back then," he recalled with a chuckle. "They must have got hard up." Horn is also distinguished as a veteran of Merrill's Marauders, a special operations jungle warfare unit of the U.S. Army that is famous for its deep penetration missions behind Japanese lines.

In the early 1940s, the minimum age for enlistment in the U.S. Army was 17, but recruits as young as 15 could enter the U.S. National Guard with their parents' permission. That was the route many young men on the Fort Belknap Reservation took. By the time the war started, most of the service age men at Fort Belknap already had left their homes.

"Everybody I knew was in the National Guard," Horn said. "Probably 90 percent of the enlistees were young like that."

After basic training in Tacoma, Wash., Horn was shuttled around to military bases from California to New Mexico. The hunting skills he'd learned growing up on the reservation served him well in the military. His commanding officers quickly learned that the young private from Montana was a crack shot with well developed tracking skills. Horn received advanced training as a sharpshooter.

"We were more sensitive to sound and stuff like that," Horn recalled of the Native American troops he served with. "I guess we had to be. We had to live by sound to get our food even."

Horn was still only 17 years old, but with more than a year of military training, he was quickly transferred from the National Guard to the regular Army. His training in cryptology was less formal than what most of the Navajo recruits underwent, but he had the advantage of speaking a Native dialect closely related to the native tongue of several other tribes from the northern plains region.

"They were not exactly the same words, but similar enough so we could converse in Indian," Horn said of his ability to speak with other Native American troops fluent in a variety of Siouxian languages. "As long as they could get two of us together — they didn't have to be both Sioux or both Assiniboine — they were close enough so we could converse."

One obstacle that had to be overcome was the fact that there were no words in Native languages for verbs and nouns commonly used in mechanized warfare. The Code Talkers had to reach agreed-upon substitutes, such as "bird" for airplane and "potato" for hand grenade.

All of Horn's training and experience with tracking, precision shooting, radio operation and translating his native language into English would soon be put to the test during one of the most dangerous and grueling Allied operations of World War II.

In the fall of 1943, Horn, now an experienced combat veteran, volunteered for service in a special operations unit preparing for combat in the South East Asian theater of World War II. The 5307th Composite Unit he joined would gain worldwide fame for its deep penetration mission into Japanese-occupied Burma.

The roughly 2,750 men who took part in the Burma campaign came to be known as Merrill's Marauders, who were so named for their commanding officer, Maj. Gen. Frank Merrill. During five months of field operations they fought the Japanese in five major engagements and 32 smaller skirmishes; they almost always faced superior forces. Gilbert Horn was right in the middle of it.

"It was a fighting unit, ready for action any time," he said of his reasons for volunteering. "I wanted to go see the war. I didn't want to be in Montana all my life. I wanted to see what's across that big waters called the oceans."

After intensive training in guerrilla warfare and jungle survival techniques, Merrill's Marauders began their mission in February 1944 with an 800-mile trek across the Himalaya Mountains and into the Burmese jungle. According to the U.S. Army Center of Military History, the Marauders' mission was to cut Japanese communications and supply lines, harasses them at every opportunity, and open the way for a planned U.S.-Chinese push to reopen a supply line into China.

They were only lightly equipped, with only the weapons and supplies they could carry on the 720 mules and horses they brought with them.

Like many veterans of his generation, Horn is reluctant to talk about the combat he experienced. He is more inclined to discuss the physical hardship the Marauders endured

"They were damn big mountains," he said of crossing the Himalayas. "We had to cut steps to get through. Those guys that had the pack animals had to make steps for their horses or mules, too."

The Marauders fought through the monsoon season, when jungle diseases and infection were at their worst. Horn remembers having to cross one river the Marauders were following 66 times. His feet were never dry.

"During the rainy season, it rained day and night continuously — just rain, rain, rain," he recalled. "You didn't have to take a shower anyway."

The Marauders consistently went on with insufficient rations, surviving on Army K-rations that were so unappetizing that most of the men threw large portions of them away. As the months passed, more and more of the Marauders were stricken with diseases such as malaria, dysentery and typhus.

Still, they fought on. The Marauders' greatest victory came in May 1944. Now down to roughly 1,300 men, the Marauders combined with elements of the Chinese 42nd and 150th Infantry regiments for an attack on a Japanese airfield at the Burmese town of Myitkyina.

Though outnumbered by a two-to-one margin, the Marauders and Chinese forces were able to take the airfield then hold-on until Chinese reinforcements arrived. But the victory came at a high price.

Of the 2,750 who had left India five months earlier, less than 200 were fit for combat when Myitkyina fell. More than 1,600 had either been killed or seriously wounded in combat. More than a 1,000 either died or had to be evacuated due to illness. Horn was wounded four times, including rounds to the chest, back and jaw.

"Very few of us came back because we were the striking units," Horn said of the Marauders' losses. "There was no support. We didn't have any artillery. They just kept on knocking us down, whittling us down. It is hard to believe what we had to go through."

The men of Merrill's Marauders have the rare distinction of having each soldier within its ranks awarded the Bronze Star. In June 1944, the 5307th Composite Unit was awarded the Distinguished Unit Citation for "gallantry, determination, and esprit de corps in accomplishing its mission under extremely difficult and hazardous conditions."

In one particularly galling act of racism, Horn remembers stopping by a local bar and seeing a sign posted on the front door reading "No Dogs or Indians Allowed." He had risked his life and his health to help free Southeast Asia from Japanese oppression, then found he still was discriminated against when he got back home.

Remarkably, all six of the Horn brothers returned from the war. True to her promise, Melvina Horn prepared herself to perform the Sun Dance in gratitude for her sons coming home to her.

Melvina Horn prayed and fasted, then cleansed herself with the fragrant smoke of sweetgrass. When she was finished, she was ready to have the flesh of her back pierced so that rawhide thongs could be passed beneath her skin and then tied to buffalo skulls laid upon the ground behind her. She would dance in a large circle for hours, dragging the heavy skulls across the earth until their weight tore the rawhide thongs from her back.

In the final moments before the dance began, Melvina turned to her son, Gilbert, and asked him to pierce her flesh.

Gilbert Horn would later tell his own children it was the hardest thing he ever had to do.[74]

Ho-Chunk Sioux

Bill Whitebear, Army; Benjamin Winneshiek, Army; Bill Mike, Army; Jesse Mike, Army; Clifford Blackdeer, Army; Emanuel Thundercloud, Army; Howard Littlejohn (KIA), Army; Alvin Blackdeer, U.S. Navy; Donald Blackdeer, U.S. Army; Irvin Blackdeer, U.S. Army; George Green, (KIA) U.S. Army; Donald Greengrass, U.S. Army; Adam Littlebear Jr., (KIA) U.S. Army; and Alfred O. Stacy, U.S. Army.

Sgt. Howard Littlejohn's job as a code talker was a very dangerous one, relaying coordinates from the front lines to another Winnebago code talker in the artillery. That meant besides knowing all the code words, Littlejohn also had to learn how to send signals in various ways, by portable field phone, radio, Morse code, and even by flag signal, if necessary. He was also required to know how to maintain and repair all the equipment. Sadly, he was killed in action, 17 April 1945.

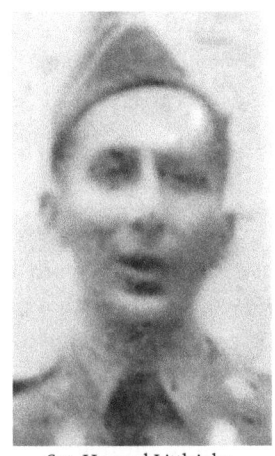

Sgt. Howard Littlejohn. www.acrossetribune.com.

Ho-Chunk Nation Code Talkers Medal. The obverse design (left) features a code talker communicating a message. Inscriptions are HO-CHUNK NATION CODE TALKERS and WOINUXAIAI HITÉTÉ, which translates to "talking secretly." The reverse design (right) features a variation of the Ho-Chunk Nation seal, which includes an eagle, bear, peace pipe and war club. An outline of Wisconsin is also included, signifying the tribe's historical attachment to the state. Inscriptions are WORLD WAR II, SOUTH PACIFIC and ACT OF CONGRESS 2008. www.usmint.gov/mint_programs/medals/?action=codeTalkers.

Fort Peck Assiniboine Sioux Tribes Code Talkers Medal (facing page). The obverse design (left) features a World War II infantry helmet and two feathers. Inscriptions are FORT PECK ASSINIBOINE, SIOUX TRIBES and CODE TALKERS. The reverse design (right) features the outline of the Fort Peck Indian Reservation (a buffalo outlined by rivers and creeks), two eagle staffs, a Plains Indian dance whip and the 41st Infantry Division patch. Inscriptions are WORLD WAR II, ACT OF CONGRESS 2008, and B CO. 1ST BN 163RD INFANTRY. www.usmint.gov/mint_programs/medals/?action=codeTalkers.

Laguna

Joseph R. Dat.

Oglala Sioux

Melvin Red Cloud, his brother William Red Cloud, Owen Brings, Garfield T. Brown and Baptiste Pumpkinseed.

When Garfield T. Brown volunteered for the Army at Fort Crook, Nebraska, in 1942, he did not realize he would play such a pivotal role in World War II and bring back an original flag of the Nazis captured in Aachen, Germany in 1944. The Oglala Lakota soldier, all 128 pounds of him, served in the 32d Field Artillery Battalion in many conflicts during World War II including North Africa, Omaha Beach, Normandy, Belgium, and the Battle of the Bulge. The family of Garfield T. Brown did not know the extent of his service during World War II. The humble "radio man" would share stories sporadically with his 11 children, … It was not until Brown passed away on 5 January 2000, when his youngest son, Richard, began to probe through his personal papers and found a "Warrior's Award" presented by the Hot Springs VA Domiciliary to Garfield Brown on 24 April 1996 "in honor of your service in World War II as a Sioux Code Talker."[75]

Cpl. Garfield Brown. www.indianz.com.

Oglala Sioux Tribe Code Talkers Medal. The obverse design (left) features a code talker with a stylized eagle in the background. Inscriptions are OGLALA and LAKOTA AKICITA IYESKA WICASA, which translates to "Indian soldier translator man." The reverse design (right) features a variation of the Oglala Sioux Tribe flag. The nine tipis represent the nine districts of Oglala—Porcupine, Wakpamni, Medicine Root, Pass Creek, Eagle Nest, White Clay, PR Village, La Creek and Wounded Knee—all of which are inscribed along the border of the design. Other inscriptions are WORLD WAR II, ACT OF CONGRESS, 2008 and AKICITA, OKOLAKICIYE, which translates to "warrior's society." www.usmint.gov/mint_programs/medals/?action=codeTalkers.

Gen Douglas MacArthur's Sioux Indian Code Talkers

Unlike the much more publicized U.S. Marine Corps Navajo Code Talker program, this smaller "Code Talker" program used Lakota, Dakota, and Nakota speaking Sioux Native American soldiers in MacArthur's South West Pacific Theater and in Europe. The program was not declassified until the mid-1970s and the U.S. Army has never seen fit to publicly recognize their Sioux code talkers to the extent that the USMC has with its Navajos. It does not fit the narrative on MacArthur.

MacArthur's Code Talker program was smaller than both the USMC program and the European Theater Comanche code talker program with the 4th Infantry Division (whose cover was blown to the Axis by the *New York Times* in 1940) and was centered around the U.S. Army's 302d Reconnaissance Squadron of the 1st Cavalry Division, a battalion sized horse cavalry reconnaissance unit, that was reorganized into two company sized units, the 302d Reconnaissance Troop (Mechanized) and the 603d Independent Tank Company. Some of the 302d code talkers graduated from the same course that the 6th Army Alamo Scout infiltration teams were selected from. The 302d had a specific Table of Organization and Equipment (TO&E) which incorporated a unique radio unit with troops of Lakota and Dakota Indian Tribes who used their ancient tribal Sioux language to communicate with other divisional headquarters troops. This secret organization, formed in the foothills of Australia and later to be known as "The Code Talkers" was recruited at the direction of General MacArthur. The close-knit group of individuals, Phillip "Stoney" LaBlanc, Edmund St. John, Baptiste Pumpkinseed, Eddie Eagle Boy, Guy Rondell, and John Bear King serving in two-man reconnaissance teams, took their task seriously. They saved many American lives using their language as an unbreakable code to fool the Japanese throughout the subsequent island campaigns. The remainder of 1943 was used for training and organizational training in Australia. As a side note of military history, the 1st Cavalry Division had Native American "Code Talkers." Like the more famous Navajo Code Talkers who served with the Marine Corps, the radio platoon of the 302d Reconnaissance Troop recruited, at the direction of General MacArthur, Lakota and Dakota Indians who used their Sioux language to communicate to other Divisional Headquarters troops.[76]

86   David M. Sullivan

The Lakota Code Talkers World War II served under Gen. MacArthur, 302nd Recon Squadron of the 1st Cavalry Division. Pictured from left to right: John Bear King, Standing Rock Sioux Tribe; Guy F. Rondell, Sisseton-Whapeton Sioux Tribe; Walter C. John, Santee Sioux Tribe; Baptiste Pumpkin Seed, Oglala Sioux Tribe; Phillip (Stoney) LaBlanc, Cheyenne River Sioux Tribe; and Edmund St John, Crow Creek Sioux Tribe. www.crstvets

Rosebud Sioux

Clarence Wolf Guts enlisted in the Army on 17 June 1942, at age eighteen, seven months after Pearl Harbor. He enlisted with his friend and cousin, Iver Crow Eagle, Sr. A captain came to his barracks and asked, "You talk Indian?" "I am Indian. One hundred percent Indian." "Well, the general wants to see you." "Me?" wondered Clarence. "What in the world did I do now?" The captain told him to get a haircut, take a shower and dress in his best clothes. He also offered tips on military etiquette: stand two feet from him, salute, say your name, rank and serial number. Then he and the captain went to see the general. "Sir, this is Clarence Wolf Guts from South Dakota," said the captain. "He talks Indian." Maj. Gen. Paul Mueller, commander of the U.S. Army's 81st Infantry, poured glasses of whiskey for the three of them, and told Clarence he wanted a man-to-man talk, "none of this 'sir' or 'general.' Just talk to me like a man." "Can you speak Indian fluently?" the general asked. Clarence said he could "read, write, and speak the Lakota Sioux language." Satisfied, the general explained that the Japanese were intercepting vital communications, and he intended to confuse them by sending messages in a Native American language. Clarence told the general, "I don't want no rank, I don't want no money. I just want to do what I can to protect America and our way of life." General Mueller said he liked his spunk. Then he asked if he knew of any other soldiers who spoke Lakota. Clarence said his cousin, Iver, was also at Camp Rucker, whereupon Mueller exclaimed, "I hit the jackpot!"

Clarence Wolf Guts. www.southdakotamagazine.com.

Two other Lakotas from South Dakota—Roy A. Bad Hand, Sr., and Benny White Bear—were also recruited. The four learned how to operate military radios, and they worked with officials to develop coded messages. They developed a phonetic alphabet and assigned military meanings to common words like turtle, tree, or horse. Their communications helped the Army to move troops and supplies without tipping off the enemy.

Clarence was General Mueller's personal code talker and traveled with him and the 81st as the division moved from island to island in the Pacific, headed for Japan. Iver accompanied the general's chief of staff. They also helped develop a phonetic alphabet based on Lakota that was later used to develop a Lakota code. When the towers of the World Trade Center fell on 11 September 2001,

88 David M. Sullivan

Clarence Wolf Guts asked his son to call the U.S. Department of Defense to see if the country needed his code talking abilities to find Osama Bin Laden. Wolf Guts was in his late 70s at the time, so his son, Don Doyle, did not make the call, but said the request personified his father's love of country. "He still wanted to help. He was trying to still be patriotic," Doyle said.[77]

Pvts. Simon Broken Leg and Jeffrey Dull Knife used their native language across their Signal Corps links while fighting in the Ardennes during the Battle of the Bulge.[78]

Rosebud Sioux Noah White Bird, Sr., Patrick McKenzie, and Anthony Omaha Boy (32d Field Artillery Battalion) also served as code talkers.

Rosebud Sioux Tribe Code Talkers Medal. The obverse design (left) depicts a World War II code talker and Sicangu Lakota warrior in profile. The code talker wears his dog tags parallel to the traditional bone-and-bead choker of the Rosebud Sioux warrior who also wears a feather in his hair. Eagle feathers are also included in the lower border of the design. Inscriptions are SICANGU LAKOTA and CODE TALKERS. The reverse design depicts the Rosebud Sioux Nation seal. Inscriptions are ROSEBUD SIOUX TRIBE, WWII, and ACT OF CONGRESS 2008. www.usmint.gov/mint_programs/medals/?action=codeTalkers.

Santee Sioux Nation Code Talkers Medal (facing page). The obverse design (left) depicts a Santee Sioux code talker looking up and focusing on the task required. The barbed wire is a symbol of the threat to the soldier. Inscriptions are MDEWAKANTON, WAKPEKUTE, and SANTEE DAKOTA SIOUX CODE TALKERS. According to the Santee Sioux Tribe, Mdewakanton translates to "dwellers at spirit lake" and wakpekute to "shooters amongst the leaves." The reverse design depicts the Santee Sioux Nation seal. Inscriptions are WORLD WAR I, WORLD WAR II and ACT OF CONGRESS 2008. ." www.usmint.gov/mint_programs/medals/?action=codeTalkers.

Santee Sioux

Walter C. John and Guy George Chapman.

Walter C. John's Dakota name was "Hok si da Shug Ya Mani" (Walking Strong Boy) and he was also known as "Cody." He attended Marty Mission Indian School, Marty, South Dakota. He entered the U.S. Army, on 15 October 1941 and began training to be a radio operator with other Lakota, Dakota, and Nakota Sioux. He served in the 302d Recon Troops, 1st Cavalry Division, in the South Pacific.[79]

Pvt. Walter C. John.
www.soiuxcityjoiurnal.com.

Charles Whitepipe, was born 7 July 1918. He grew up around Bad Nation and attended the Pierre Indian Boarding School and then graduated valedictorian from Mission High School. He began school at Whapeton School of Science in electrical engineering when he was inducting into military service in 1941. He was already in training in California when Pearl Harbor was attacked. The following day, he shipped out to Hawaii. From Hawaii his unit was sent to the Pacific island of New Guinea. It was in New Guinea when another soldier from Sioux Falls told his commanding officer that Charlie Whitepipe would make a good forward observer because—in his words—"the Sioux are stealthy, sneaky, people." The characterization angered Whitepipe, but it apparently impressed his commanding officer. Charlie Whitepipe spent the next two years in New Guinea as a forward observer and radio man, moving ahead of his unit and communicating in Lakota with a ship-based partner to direct artillery fire at enemy troops. In 1944, he was shipped home suffering from malaria and jungle rot, the result of months spent in water-filled foxholes.

SISSETON-WAHPETON SIOUX

Guy F. Rondell

Sgt. Guy F. Rondell, a Lakota from the Sisseton-Wahpeton Sioux Tribe of South Dakota, was a graduate of the second Alamo Scouts training class and returned to the 302d Recon Squadron of the 1st Cavalry Division. He was one of only eleven Lakota speaking Sioux code talkers that served during the war. Six served in the Pacific and five in Europe.[80]

Sisseton Wahpeton Oyate Code Talkers Medal. The obverse design (left) depicts a soldier being shielded by an eagle to keep him safe. Inscriptions are SISSETON WAHPETON SIOUX and DAKOTA CODE TALKERS. "Dakota" is the dialect used by the tribe. The reverse design features a variation of the Sisseton Wahpeton Oyate Tribe seal. The central part of the design depicts the boundaries of the reservation with seven tipis, which represent the seven districts within the Sisseton Wahpeton Oyate of Lake Traverse Reservation. Inscriptions are PACIFIC THEATRE, WORLD WAR II, LAKE TRAVERSE RESERVATION and ACT OF CONGRESS 2008. www.usmint.gov/mint_programs/medals/?action=codeTalkers.

Standing Rock Sioux

John Bear King.

Standing Rock Sioux Tribe Code Talkers Medal. The obverse design (left) features code talkers transmitting and writing information. Inscriptions are LAKOTA CODE TALKERS and STANDING ROCK SIOUX TRIBE. The reverse design features the seal of the Standing Rock Sioux Tribe. Inscriptions include PORCUPINE, LONG SOLDIER, CANNON BALL, WAKPALA, KENEL, RUNNING ANTELOPE, BEAR SOLDIER and ROCK CREEK, the eight districts of the Standing Rock Sioux Tribe. Additional inscriptions are ACT OF CONGRESS 2008, STANDING ROCK SIOUX TRIBE, JULY 1873, WORLD WAR I and WORLD WAR II. www.usmint.gov/mint_programs/medals/?action=codeTalkers.

Yankton Sioux

There are no known World War I Yankton Sioux code talkers. However, and despite the medal is inscribed World War I, the medals were awarded to brothers Daniel and Rufus Ross, obviously veterans of World War II.

Daniel and Rufus Ross. www.indianz.com.

Yankton Sioux Tribe Code Talkers Medal. The obverse design (left) features two code talkers with the inscriptions YANKTON SIOUX and CODE TALKERS. The reverse design (right) features a variation of the buffalo skull painted in honor of Yankton Sioux Tribe veterans. It is inscribed with WORLD WAR I. www.usmint.gov/mint_programs/medals/?action=codeTalkers.

Tlingit

Robert Jeff David, Harvey Jacobs, Mark Jacobs, Jr., George V. Lewis, and Richard Bean, Sr.

Mark Jacobs, Jr., served as a quartermaster 3/c in the U.S. Navy. During four years of military service, nearly all of which were sea duty and in war zones, he served on the USS *New Mexico* in the Aleutians and on the USS *Newberry*, the last two years served in the Amphibious Forces in the South Pacific. He and his brother, Harvey, never attended basic training and were immediately put to work on "picket boats" in the Icy Straits area. Using "code," he and his brother Harvey were part of a group of lesser-known code talkers, communicating only in the Tlingit language. Jacobs witnessed the flag raising on Mt. Suribachi on Iwo Jima and recorded it in the ship's log; witnessed the second (larger) flag raising as well. He was also in the Okinawa and other campaigns.[81]

Tlingit Tribe Code Talkers Medal. On the obverse design (left), the antenna on the soldier's equipment is raised as he talks on his radio sending a coded message. The soldier kneels on his right knee and holds his rifle in his left hand in case of attack. The three semicircles signify the transmission of radio signals. It is inscribed TLINGIT WARRIORS CODE TALKERS. The reverse design (right) depicts a killer whale headdress representing the Tlingit code talkers of World War II who were affiliated with the Killer Whale Clan. Inscriptions are WORLD WAR II, KILLER WHALE CLAN and ACT OF CONGRESS 2008. www.usmint.gov/mint_programs/medals/?action=codeTalkers.

Unknown Sioux Tribal Affiliation

John C. Smith served in the 32d Field Artillery Battalion.

Tonto Apache

Paul Burdette. The name "Apache" is typed in right below Paul Burdette as one of the nine names typed in a circle matrix bearing his code name, "Rebel," which was a top secret in the records of the U.S. Army during his service, which began on 10 November 1942 until he was honorably discharged on 25 November 1945. He served as a gunner on a B-24 nicknamed "Doodlebug." Since the code talkers had worked in teams of two, his partner was Nelson Danford, a member of the White Mountain Apache Tribe. His code name was "Tarter." Other code names listed in the matrix were, "Archer," "Chesnut," "Badger," "Henchman," "Douling," "Hit-Day," and "Gangway."[82] Unfortunately, the Apache of the 380th Bomb Group associated with these code names have yet to be determined.

Tonto Apache Tribe Code Talkers Medal. The obverse design (left) depicts a close-up and background view of a code talker, which represents communicating a message and running a message. Inscriptions are TONTO APACHE TRIBE and CODE TALKERS. The reverse design (right) features a variation of the Tonto Apache seal, which depicts four feathers, a streak of stylized lightning as depicted in Apache art and four streamers. Inscriptions are WORLD WAR I and ACT OF CONGRESS 2008. www.usmint.gov/mint_programs/medals/?action=codeTalkers

White Mountain Apache

Nelson Danford, "Tarter," served in the 380th Bomb Group in the South Pacific.

White Mountain Apache Tribe Code Talkers Medal. The obverse design (left) features code talkers behind sand bags. The code talker in the foreground is using a field phone to deliver a message, while the one in the background writes the coded message. Inscriptions are WHITE MOUNTAIN APACHE TRIBE and CODE TALKERS. The reverse design (right) features a variation of the White Mountain Apache Tribe seal. The seal depicts a rainbow rising against the sky over a landscape with an elk standing by a river near a wikiup, or traditional dwelling. Snow-capped mountains are in the distance, while nearer, at the base of the seal, is a pine forest. An earthen Apache vase, in the foreground, is flanked by two feathers and a pair of lightning bolts near the outer edge of the seal. Inscriptions are WORLD WAR II and ACT OF CONGRESS 2008. www.usmint.gov/mint_programs/medals/?action=codeTalkers.

When consulted with regard to the recipients of the Code Talker medals, the US Army Center of Military History, Carlisle, Pennsylvania, replied:

> There were no specific units in which most of the Code Talkers served in the Army. Unlike the Marine Corps, who formed a specific organization for Navajo Code talkers, the Army tended to be more decentralized. We often relied on the tribal councils to provide information, with final decisions, in questionable cases, sometimes coming down to determining that a Native American served overseas in a combat unit. Many of these involved local commanders employing them as communications personnel in an ad hoc manner. In the end, for various reasons, we tended to defer to the tribal councils when they submitted a name, interpreting the Congressional guidance somewhat liberally. This should not be taken to denigrate anyone's service, it just indicates that after more than seventy years in the case of World War II and 100 in the case of World War I, the records are not as clear and concise as we might wish. All who received medals served honorably.

He added:

> There are four or five tribes that will be getting the Congressional Commemorative Medal in the future.

Notes

1. www.bbc.com/news/magazine-26963624.
2. www.twcnews.com/archives/tx/austin/2007/09/17/texas-military-honors-choctaw-code-talkers-TX_192100.old.html.
3. The Code Talkers Recognition Act of 2008 (Act) (Public Law 110-420) requires the Secretary of the Treasury to strike Congressional Medals in recognition of the dedication and valor of Native American code talkers to the U.S. Armed Services during World War I and World War II. "Code talkers" refers to those Native Americans who used their tribal languages as a means of secret communication during wartime. Under the Act, unique gold medals are struck for each Native American tribe that had a member who served as a code talker. Silver duplicate medals are presented to the specific code talkers, their next of kin, or other personal representatives. In addition, bronze duplicates are available for sale to the public
4. www.childrenofthesunnativeculture.com.
5. In President Ronald Reagan's Proclamation 4954—National Navaho Code Talkers Day, 28 July 1982, the following is noted, "It is fitting that at this time we also express appreciation for the other American Indians who have served our Nation in times of war. Members of the Choctaw, Chippewa, Creek, Sioux, and other tribes used their tribal languages as effective battlefield codes against the Germans in World War I and the Japanese and Germans in World War II."
6. David, Kahn, *The Codebreakers: The Story of Secret Writing* (New York: MacMillan Co., 1967), 550. Another source credits Chief George Baconrind as heading the detail.
7. World War I and II Choctaw Code Takers, www.oklachahta.org/Code%20Talkers.htm.
8. Alfred Wainwright Bloor (1876-1952) graduated from the State Agricultural and Mechanical College of Texas, served as a sergeant in the First Texas Militia from 1895 until 1898, and served with Company L of the First Texas Volunteer Infantry in the Spanish-American War from 11 May 1898 until 20 April 1899. After the war, he remained in the Texas National Guard in various positions until World War I. In 1914, he was appointed lieutenant colonel of the 2d Texas Infantry and served on the Mexican border in 1916. In 1917, he received an appointment as colonel of the 7th Texas Infantry Regiment, a unit being raised for service in World War I. Colonel Bloor recruited the regiment throughout North and Northwest Texas. The federal government drafted the regiment into service in August 1917, and sent it to Camp Bowie, Texas, in September 1917. At Camp Bowie, the War Department merged the 7th Texas with the 1st Oklahoma Infantry. The new organization became the 142d Infantry Regiment, and Colonel Bloor retained command of the new regiment. After training at Camp Bowie until June of 1918, Colonel Bloor led his regiment overseas to France as part of the 36th Infantry Division. On 8 October 1918, he led his regiment into combat for the first time during the Battle of St. Etienne in the Champagne region. In its first combat experience, the regiment suffered greatly, with casualties of eight officers and 111 men killed on that day. After St. Etienne, Bloor saw his regiment through the battle of Forest Ferme on 27 October 1918, in which the 142d Infantry overran German positions in under an hour and suffered casualties of eight men killed and sixteen men wounded. After the armistice, Colonel Bloor remained in command of his regiment and in May of 1919 led it back to Camp Bowie, where the Texan and Oklahoman soldiers were demobilized. He was honored with the Croix de Guerre for his "gallantry in action, tshaonline.org/handbook/online/articles/fbl75.
9. Choctaw Indian Code Talkers of World War I, www.texasmilitaryforcesmuseum.org/choctaw/codetalkers.htm.
10. www.texasmilitaryforcesmuseum.org/choctaw/codetalkers.htm.
11. Capt. Ben H. Chastaine, *The Story of the 36th: The Experiences of the 36th Division in the World War* (Oklahoma City, OK: Harlow Publishing Co., 1920), 231–232.
12. In November 1917, Company E of the 142d consisted of 208 Native Americans from fourteen tribes from Oklahoma: 89 Choctaws, 68 Cherokees, 15 Chickasaws, 7 Osages, 7 Creeks, 6 Seminoles, 5

Delawares, 2 Shawnees, 2 Quapaws, 2 Poncas, 2 Caddos, 1 Peoria, 1 Arapaho, and 1 Cheyenne. William C. Meadows, *The Comanche Code Talkers of Word War II* (Austin, TX: University of Texas Press, 2002),15, (hereafter Meadows, *Comanche Code Talkers*).

13. Choctaw Indian Code Talkers of World War I, www.texasmilitaryforcesmuseum.org/choctaw/codetalkers.htm. For Leader's service with Company B, 2d Machine Gun Battalion, 16th Infantry Regiment, 1st Infantry Division, see , Otis Leader, "Horrors of the Western Front," *Journal of Chickasaw History and Culture*, 10, no, 3, Ser, 37 (2004): 4-21, and 10. no. 3, Ser.39 (2004): 4-25.

14. Ibid.

15. *Bishinik* (the Choctaw Nation newspaper published in Durant, OK), April 1987,

16. Ibid.

17. Ibid.

18. s3.amazonaws.com/choctaw-msldigital/assets/512/codetalkerhandout_original.

19. *Canku Ota,*A Newsletter Celebrating Native America, 3 June 2000-Issue 11, turtletrack.org/Issues00/Co06032000/CO_06032000_Codetalk.htm.

20. Duane K. Hale, "Forgotten Heroes: American Indians in World War I," *Four Winds*, 3, no. 2 (1982): 38-41.

21. www.cherokee.org.

22. Meadows, *Comanche Code*, 29.

23. Ibid.

24. www.kswo.com/story/18909740/an-original-code-talker-is-honored-by-the-comanche-nation.

25. www.badeagle.com/cgi-bin/ib3/cgi-bin/ikonboard.cgi?act=Print;f=77;t=13386.

26. "Bear Ghost, Alphonse," *Mathers Museum of World Cultures Digital Exhibits*, dlib.indiana.edu/omeka/mathers/items/show/302.

27. www.nd.gov/veterans/heroes/richard-blue-earth.

28. "Two Horses, Edward," *Mathers Museum of World Cultures Digital Exhibits*, accessed 27 May 2016, http://dlib.indiana.edu/omeka/mathers/items/show/334.

29. *American Indian Magazine*, 7, no. 2 (Summer 1919): 101.

30. Thomas A. Britten, *American Indians in World War I* (Albuquerque: University of New Mexico Press, 1997), 107.

31. www.osagenation-nsn.gov/news-events/news/wwi-osage-code-talker-be-honored-veterans-day.

32. www.usmint.gov/mint_programs/medals.

33. Lawrence Stallings, *The Doughboys: The Story of the AEF, 1917–1918* (New York: Harper & Row, Publishers, 1963), 288.

34. www. about/cryptologic_heritage/museum/virtual_tour/museum_tour_text.shtml.

35. www.kswo.com/story/18909740/an-original-code-talker-is-honored-by-the-comanche-nation.

36. Meadows, *Comanche Code Talkers*, 65.

37. W, Preston Corderman, Colonel, Signal Corps, to Colonel McCormick, 8 September 1943, as quoted in William C. Meadows, *The Comanche Code Talkers of World War II* (Austin; University of Texas Press, 2002), 41–42.

38. www.cherokee.org/News/Stories/32170.aspx.

39. Gary Robinson, *The Language of Victory: American Indian Code Talkers of World War I and World War II* (Bloomington, IN: iUniverse, 2011), 29–30, (hereafter Robinson, *Language of Victory*).

40. Ibid.
41. www.ww2f.com/topic/15837-the-platoon-that-suckered-the-siegfried-line.
42. *Bishinik,* July 1986, 2. Billy was the last surviving Choctaw code talker.
43. Information received from *Bishinik,* 14 November 2016.
44. Meadows, *Comanche Code Talkers,* 29,
45. Ibid., 74–77.
46. Ibid., 79.
47. Ibid., 89.
48. Ibid., 95.
49. comanchemuseum.com/code_talkers.
50. Ibid.
51. soldiers.dodlive.mil/tag/meuse-argonne-offensive.
52. soldiers.dodlive.mil/tag/code-talkers.
53. marine73110.tripod.com/id20.html.
54. Robinson, *The Language of Victory,* 77–78.
55. Meadows, *The Comanche Code Talkers,* 81
56. Robinson, *The Language of Victory,* 85.
57. Ibid.
58. www.bozemandailychronicle.com/100/newsmakers/barney-old-coyote-warrior-educator-indian-rights-advocate/article.
59. Meadows, *The Comanche Code Talkers,* 69.
60. www.cookcountynews-herald.com/news/2013-12-14/General_News/Lex_Porter_honored_for_service_as_Code_Talker.html.
61. Meadows, *The Comanche Code Talkers,* 68.
62. usatoday30.usatoday.com/news/nation/2002/07/06/codetalkers.htm.
63. www.msswarriors.org/history/MeskinteractiveCD1/Pages/Culture/WarriorsWWIICodeTalkers.htm, accessed 13 October 2016.
64. theadventuresofbillymax.blogspot.com/2012/08/meskwaki-code-talkers.html.
65. www.mymalonetelegram.com/mtg01/last-surviving-wwii-akwesasne-mohawk-code-talker-awarded-congressional-silver-medal.
66. www.postcrescent.com/story/news/2014/05/25/honor-code-/9581163.
67. www.brummettechohawkproject.com.
68. www.seminolenationmuseum.org/m.blog/23/seminole-code-talker.
69. www.sdlegislature.gov/sessions/2002/bills/HC1026p.
70. www.angelfire.com/sd2/corsoncounty/WW_II_1943_.html.
71. sd.ng.mil/News/Press%20Releases/151104.
72. www.wolfpointherald.com/index.php/cs-news/local-news/1981-code-talkers-honored-posthumously.
73. Meadows, *The Comanche Code Talkers,* 70, citing *Indian Country Today,* 8 June 1994.
74. www.greatfallstribune.com/story/news/2014/01/05/code-talker/4311455.

75. www.indianz.com/News/2015/019092.asp?print=1
76. chicagoboyz.net/archives/36899.html. See, also, this 1st Cavalry Division Association link (http://www.first-team.us/tableaux/chapt_02/) on the 1st Cavalry's "Sioux Code Talkers"; www.crstvets.org/code-talkers; and http://www.militaryvetshop.com/History/1stCavalry.html.
77. genealogytrails.com/sdak/codetalkers.html.
78. Meadows, *The Comanche Code Talkers*, 70.
79. www.crstvets.org/code-talkers.
80. www.alamoscouts.org/features/war_stories/warrior_spirit, as mentioned in http://chicagoboyz.net/archives/36899.html.
81. www.rootsweb.ancestry.com.
82. "Apache Code Talker Honored at U.S. Capitol," www.pechanga.net/content/apache-code-talker-honored-us-capitol.

Index

1st Infantry, Oklahoma National Guard	16, 18
Adair, Pvt. George	*21*
Adams, Charles	79
Adams, Matt D.	79
Adams, Rupert S.	67
Akwesasne Mohawk Code Talkers Medal	65
Alverez, Joseph R.	79
Arquette, Pvt. Mike	62
Atchavit, Pvt. Calvin	22, 23, *24*
Baker, Pfc. Forrester	38
Band Hand, Roy A. Sr.	87
Barnes, Pfc. Joseph	62
Battle of Saint-Mihiel	22
Battle of St. Lo	49
Battle of the Bulge	49, 63, 84, 88, 89
Bean, Richard, Sr.	93
Bear Ghost, Cpl. Alphonse	23, 26, *27*
Bear King, John	75, 85, *86*, 90
Bear Shield, Julius	25
Bear, Everett D.	79
Becker, Professor W. G.	43
Belgarde, Arthur	79
Belgarde, Dominick	79
Belgarde, Herman	79
Benson, Edward	59, *61*
Big Horn Elk, Louis	25
Billy, 2d Lt. Schlicht	38, *39*, 40-41
Billy, Pfc. Albert	9, *10*, 11
Birdinground, Samson	52
Blackdeer, Clifford	93
Bloor, Col. A. W.	8-9
Blue Earth, Pvt. Richard	25, *28*
Bobb, Pvt. Mitchell	5, *7*, 11, *22*
Brave Bull, Pvt. John	25, *30*
Broken Leg, Pvt. Simon	75, 88
Brought Plenty, August	25
Brown, Cpl. Garfield T.	*84*
Brown, Cpl. Victor	11, *15*
Buck Elk, Harvey	79

Burdette, Paul	94
Bush, President George W.	1
Cantigny, France	12
Cantrell, Archie, M.	79
Cantrell, John	79
Carterby, Pvt. Ben	5, 11, *19*
Chapella, Frank	55
Chapman, Guy George	36, 89
Charles Lazore	62
Chastaine, Capt. Ben H.	9
Cherokee Nation Code Talkers Medal	*26*
Chevalier de L'Ordre National du Merite	*41*
Cheyenne River Sioux Tribe Code Talkers Medal	*76*
Chibbity, Cpl. Charles	42, *43*, *44*, 45, *46*, 47, *48*, 49, 50-51
Choctaw Medal of Valor for World War I	*19*
Choctaw Medal of Valor	17
Choctaw Nation Code Talkers Medal	*21*
Chouteau Jones, Frances	35
Chouteau, Augustus	35
Clark, Pvt. George	22, *25*, 37
Codynah, Haddon	22, 42, *44*
Coffman, Napanee Brown	15
Colbert, Pvt. Benjamin, Jr.	11
Cole, Pvt. Thomas	62
Comanche Nation Code Talkers Medal	*51*
Connors, Louis Stanley	62
Conwoop, Pvt. Gilbert Pahdi	22, *23*
Cook, Pfc. Angus B.	62
Cozad, Leonard Sr.	57
Crow Creek Tribe Code Talkers Medal	*78*
Crow Nation Code Talkers Medal	*53*
Crow Necklace, Thomas	25
Crow Skin, Louis	25
Crow, Eagle, Iver, Sr.	75, 87
Danford, Nelson	94, 95
Dann, Pvt. Floyd, Sr.	*55*
Davenport, Pfc. George	11, *22*
Davenport, Pvt. Joseph	11
David, Robert Jeff	93
Davis, SSgt. Frank	68

Dawson, Mozelle	9, 10
Dickens, Sgt. Davis	38
Doxtater, Cpl. Hudson	67
Doxtater, Rimton, L.	67
Dull Knife. Pvt. Jeffrey	88
Dupree, Duncan	79
Eagle Boy, Eddie	75, 77, 85, 86
Eagle Chasing, Narcisse	77
Echohawk, Sgt. Brummett	68, 70
Eder, James J.	78
Edwards, Cpl. James, Sr.	11, 14-16, 22
Elk Horn, Moses	36
Elk, John	25
Fond du Lac Band of Lake Superior Chippewa Tribe Code Talkers Medal	54
Fort Peck Assiniboine Sioux Tribes Code Talkers Medal	82
Fort Sill Indian School, Lawton, Oklahoma	47
Frazier, Cpl. Tobias William	11
Good Iron, Paul	25
Gover, Sgt. Grant	69
Gover, SSgt. Philip	69
Grass, Pvt. Albert	25, 31
Gray Bull. Thomas	25
Gray Day, Joseph	25
Gray Hawk, Pvt. Benjamin	26, 34
Halsey, George Jacob	25
Halsey, Michael	25
Hamilton, Joseph	79
Hampton, Pvt. Benjamin Wilburn	11
Harjo, Pvt. Edmund	72, 73
Haskell Indian School, Lawrence, Kansas	44, 45
Hawk, William	79
Histia, SSgt. Paul R.	71
Ho-Chunk Nation Code Talkers Medal	83
Holder, Robert	42, 44
Hollow, Anton	79
Honani, Perry, Sr.	54
Hopi Tribe Code Talkers Medal	57
Horn, Gilbert, Sr.	79-82
Horn, Melvina	82

Hurtgen Forest	49
Iron Elk, Willie	36
Jacobs, Harvey	93
Jacobs, QM 3/c Mark, Jr.	93
Jim, Enoch	69
John, Pvt. Walter C.	75, *89*
Johnson, President Lyndon B.	53
Johnson, Pvt., Noel	11, *20*
Jones, Earl	79
Jones, Frank	79
Jones, Ralph N.	79
Kassanavoid, Forrest	37, 42, 50
King, Pfc., Louis E.	62
King, Pvt., Joe	62
Kiowa Tribe Code Talkers Medal	*57*
Kirn, Jay H.	79
Koiyaquaptewa, Warren	55
LaBlanc, Pvt. Phillip "Stoney"	75, *77*, 85, *86*
Lambert, Barney	79
Lambert, Joseph	79
Laughing, Angus J.	62
Lazore, Pfc. Alex W.	62
Leader, Cpl. Otis	11, 12-13
Lean Elk, Pvt. Harvey E.	26, *34*
Left Hand Thunder, Richard	79
Lewis, George V.	93
Little Chief, Pvt. Charles	25, *32*
Little Head, Ben	79
Littlejohn, Sgt. Howard	*83*
Lomakema, Charles	55
Lone Star Medal of Valor	2
Long Tree, Mark	79
Longee, Louis E.	79
Louis, Cpl. Solomon Bond	5, 6, 11, 16, *17*, 22
MacArthur, Douglas	85
Marty Mission Indian School, Marty, South Dakota	89
Mason, Jesse, Jr.	79
Matchapatow, William	58
Mathapotow, Dave	58
Matlock, SSgt. Chauncey	69

Maytubby, Cpl. Peter	5, 11
McGhee, Bonnie	78
McIntosh, Thomas	66
McKenzie, Patrick	88
Melbourne, James M., Jr.	79
Melton, William	72
Menominee Nation Code Talkers Medal	58
Merrill's Marauders	80, 81, 82
Meskwaki Nation Code Talkers Medal	61
Meuse-Argonne Offensive	15, 35
Mihecoby, Wellington	42, 44
Mike, Bill	83
Mike, Jesse	83
Molas, George	25
Molash, David	25
Morgan, Sgt. Harold	69
Muscogee Creek Nation Code Talkers Medal	66
Nahquaddy, Albert, Jr.	42, 45
Nahquaddy, Pvt., Edward Albert, Sr.	22, 23
Navajo	1, 44, 75, 85
Navenma, Percival	55
Nelson, Pvt. Jeff	11
Not Afraid, Cyril	52
Noyabad, Perry	42, 50
O'Katchekum, John C.	58
Oakes, Pvt. Alex	62
Oakes, T/5 Louis L.	62, 63
Oglala Sioux Tribe Code Talkers Medal	84
Ogle, Raymond L.	79
Ogle, William G.	79
Oklahombe, Pfc. Joseph	11, 12, 14, 15
Old Coyote, Barney Jr.	52-53
Old Coyote, Henry	52
Omaha Boy, Anthony	88
Oneida Nation Code Talkers Medal	66
Operation Market Garden	63
Osage Nation Code Talkers Medal	68
Otitivo, Clifford	42, 44
Paddlety, Jim	57
Palmer, Cpl. Tony	72, 74

Parker, Simmons	42, 43, 44
Pawnee Nation Code Talkers Medal	68
Permansu, Melvin	42
Perry, Cpl. Andrew	38
Pershing, General John	13
Petain, Marshal of France Henri	13
Peters, Alex W.	62
Philip Johnston	1, 44
Pike, Joe Harry	62
Ponca Tribe Code Talkers Medal	*71*
Pooyouma, Sgt. Rex	55, *56*
Porter, Freedom	54
Porter, Lex C.	54
Pretends Eagle, Joseph	25
Pueblo of Acoma Code Talkers Medal	*71*
Pumpkinseed. Baptiste	75, 84, 85, *86*
Reagan, President Ronald	1
Red Bean, John	25
Red Boy, Archie	79
Red Boy, Shirley Q.	79
Red Cloud, Melvin	84
Red Dog, Lawrence	79
Red Elk, Elgin	*42, 44*
Red Elk, Gerald	79
Red Elk, Herman, Jr.	79
Red Elk, Roderick	42, 44, 45, 49-50
Red Fox, William J.	79
Red Fox. George James	25
Red Stone, Asa	25
Red, Cloud, William	84
Redd, Adam	79
Reddoor, Joseph	78, 79
Rice, MSgt. Floyd	69
Richards, Leslie	66
Roberts, Dewey	59, *61*
Rondell, Sgt. Guy	75, 85, 86, 89
Roosevelt, Theodore, Jr.	48
Roosevelt, Theodore, Sr.	5
Rosebud Sioux Tribe Code Talkers Medal	88
Ross, Daniel	*92*

Ross, Rufus	92
Russell, Joseph E.	79
Sanache, Frank	59, *61*
Sanache, Pvt. Willard	*59, 61*
Santee Sioux Nation Code Talkers Medal	89
Santee. George W.	25
Saupitty, Larry	42, 44, 47
Schuyler, Lloyd	67
Second Battle of the Somme	5
See the Elk, Lawrence	25
Seminole Nations Code Talkers Medal	*75*
Shields, Julian	79
Shupla, Franklin	55
Siegfried Line	38, 40, 41, 49
Sisseton Wahpeton Oyate Code Talkers Medal	90
Sleeps from Home, George	25
Smith, John C.	94
Snake, William I.	71
Speaks, Walking, Luke	26, 35
St. John, Edmund	75, 78, 85, *86*
Standing Bear, Clyde	25, 79
Standing Rock Sioux Tribe Code Talkers Medal	*91*
Stoneroad, Henry C., Jr.	69
Sunday, Mitchell P.	62
Sunrise, Morris	42, 44
Swift Eagle, Gregory B.	79
Tabbyetchy, Morris	42
Tabbytite, Anthony	42
Tabytosavit, Pvt. Samuel	22, *25*
Tarbell, Albert	62, 63, *64, 65*
Tarbell, Mitchell	63
Tattoed, James	25
Taylor, Pvt. Robert	*11*
Thundercloud, Emanuel	83
Tlingit Tribe Code Talkers Medal	92
Tonto Apache Tribe Code Talkers Medal	93
Traversie, Alexander	25
Treadwell, Maj. Jack	l, 38
Tsatoke, John	57
Twain, Malvin "Mike"	59, *61*

Two Bears, George — 25
Two Bears, Joseph — 25
Two Horses, Pvt. Edward — 25, 26, 28, 29
U.S. Army Organizations
    1st Cavalry Division — 69, 77, 85, 89, 90
    1st Infantry Division — 12, 26
    2d North Dakota Volunteer Infantry — 26
    4th Infantry Division — 44, 45, 48, 49, 85
    4th Signal Company — 44
    5th Army Air Corps — 55
    5th Cavalry Regiment — 67
    16th Infantry Regimen — 12
    18th Infantry Regiment — 26
    26th Infantry Regiment — 26
    32d Field Artillery Battalion — 88
    32d Infantry Division — 67
    32d Infantry Regiment — 54
    33d Infantry Division — 69
    34th "Red Bull" Division — 59
    36th Infantry Division — 5
    41st Infantry Division — 79
    45th Infantry Division — 38, 69
    57th Field Artillery Brigade — 54
    81st Infantry Division — 55
    82d Airborne Division — 48, 62
    90th Infantry Division — 23
    101st Airborne Division — 48, 62
    141st Infantry Regiment — 11
    142d Infantry Regiment — 5, 11
    143d Infantry Regiment — 5, 11
    157th Infantry Regiment — 69
    163d Infantry Regiment — 79
    168th Infantry — 59
    179th Infantry Regiment — 69
    180th Infantry Regiment — 38, 69
    302d Reconnaissance Troop (Mechanized) — 85, 89, 90
    357th Infantry Regiment — 23
    380th Bombardment Group — 55, 94
    442d Signal Battalion — 62
    527th Field Artillery Battalion — 67

603d Independent Tank Company	85
689th Field Artillery Battalion	57
Alamo Scouts	85
U.S. Marine Corps	1, 37, 44, 85
USS *New Mexico*	93
USS *Newberry*	93
Utah Beach, Normandy	47, 48, 49
Veach, Capt. Columbus Walter	11, 16, *18*
Vogel, Clayton B, Major General, USMC)	1
Wabaunasee, Judie Wayne	59, 60, *61*
Wabaunasee, Mike Wayne	59, *61*
Wadsworth, Cpl. Orville	*55*
Wahnee, Bessie,	51
Wahnee, Ralph	42, 51
Waupoose, Dan	*58*
Wausakokamick, Mose	58
White Bear, Benny	87
White Bear, Bill	83
White Bird, Noah, Sr.	88
White Eagle, Richard	26
White Eagle, Roscoe	25
White Lightning, Paul	26
White Mountain Apache Tribe Code Talkers Medal	95
White Pipe, Charles	86
White, Pfc. Reginald	62
Wilson, Cpl. Calvin	11, *22*
Wilson, Winfield	79
Winneshiek, Benjamin	83
Wolf Guts, Clarence	*87*-88
Yacheschi, Willis	42, *44*, 50, 51
Yaiva, Travis	55
Yankton Sioux Tribe Code Talkers Medal	92
Yellow Owl, James T.	79
Young Bear, Frank	26
Young Bear, Pvt. Dewey	59, 60, *61*
Young Man, Douglas	77
Zahn, Pvt. Francis Benjamin	26, *33*